My Covent Garden

DEDICATED

TO THE MEMORY

OF

SIR BRONSON ALBERY

———

A THEATRE MANAGER
OF VAST EXPERIENCE,
EXCEPTIONAL COURTESY,
AND RARE ENLIGHTENMENT

£2·00

DELETED

ALAN DENT

My Covent Garden

With 40 illustrations and a map

London

J. M. Dent & Sons Limited

Made in Great Britain
at the
Aldine Press · Letchworth   Herts
for
J. M. DENT & SONS LTD
Aldine House · Bedford Street · London

ISBN 0 460 04112 6

CONTENTS

ILLUSTRATIONS

Map, p. viii

Between pages 82 and 83

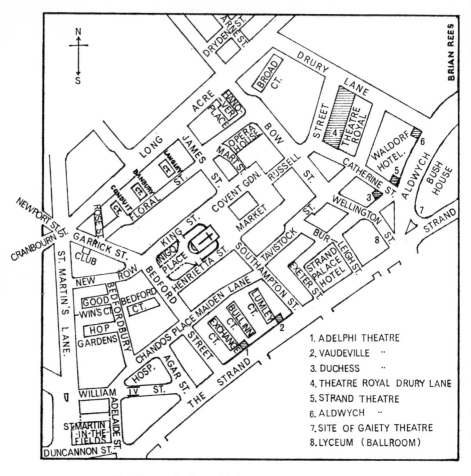

My Covent Garden, with St Paul's Church at its heart.

FORE-PIECE

It must be part of the Londoner's innate and almost mystical perversity to have decided to call the quarter 'Covent Garden' instead of the Convent Garden, which it historically was. Innumerable books, essays and pamphlets on the subject tell us that the name *was* so changed (instead of telling us *how* and *why*): 'The name of the place was originally Convent Garden, from an old garden of the monks of Westminster Abbey which stretched from Long Acre to the Strand', etc., etc.

It is an accepted fact that the workaday Glaswegian elides the letter *t* unless it begins the word (he elides it even in the words 'Scotland' and 'Scottish'). It is no less accepted that the Cockney cannot make the letter *h* other than mute, whether at the beginning or anywhere else in the word. But no theory of literary elision can explain why the first *n*—and the first *n* only—has come to be dropped from a simple word like 'convent' both in its spelling and in its pronunciation. This is inexplicable, but it just *is* so—just as asparagus and cucumbers were 'sparrowgrass' and 'cowcumbers' to the Covent Garden marketeer long, long before Charles Dickens created his Sairey Gamp; and they are still so called.

Another fascinating and equally inexplicable fact is the rare but occasional occurrence of the version 'Common Garden' for Covent Garden. This occurs more than once in Samuel Pepys, for example when the diarist is in search of an artist to paint his wife's miniature portrait, and goes 'by coach to Common-Garden Coffee-house' to find 'Mr. Cooper, the great painter' who lived in Henrietta Street (see entry for 30th March 1667-8).

This version also occurs, more than once, in the play by R. L. Stevenson and W. E. Henley called *Deacon Brodie* (set in the year

1780) when the Edinburgh rogue is visited and rounded-up by the Bow Street Runner called Mr Hunt, whose address in London is explicitly stated to be 'King Street, Common Garden'.

Covent Garden Market—Common Garden? From this variant it occurs to me—now writing in England at the end of the twentieth century—that the next step may be to call the dear old place 'The Common Market', and have done with it! For so long as it remains a Market.

CHAPTER ONE

THE GARDEN OF MY HEART

My title—at the outset—should not be taken to imply that this, the heart of central London, is my property, in the material sense in which it was once the property of the Dukes of Bedford. It should, rather, be taken to imply that Covent Garden belongs to me in the spiritual sense, very much in the way that Glasgow used to belong to the late Will Fyffe in the best of his songs (for one day in the week at least, and when he had adequately refreshed himself).

Covent Garden is part of my very nature, and for one of my Bohemian character it is the very core of London, just as Mayfair is the core of London for the man-about-town, and just as the East End is the only end that matters to the true Cockney. I have spent at least fifteen years of my life residing in the middle of Covent Garden—five of them in Long Acre and ten of them in King Street. So I belong to Covent Garden, and find myself in it every time I go to London.

A scrap of autobiography is essential here. I was born in the first week of January 1905, the third and youngest child of a gracious-looking but (by me) unremembered mother, who died when I was only two. This should explain why my father and my dear sister, who was nine years older than I, did their best to comfort me by lavishing too much love on me and—in short—spoiling me for the rest of their lives.

From the first I was a moody little customer, fond of solitude and solitary walks, and not much inclined to play with my schoolmates unless when I could induce them to play at play-acting. For I had from my earliest years a passion for the theatre, which is rather hard to explain in an infant born and reared in a little town more than forty miles south of Glasgow. My father, a delightful and rather Micawberish character, did nothing to discourage these histrionic tendencies in his youngest and best-beloved. He used to be obliged, in the course of one of his many businesses, to go to Glasgow by rail every Thursday morning. Often he would take me with him, to the matinée at the Pavilion Music Hall at the top of Renfield Street. As a result of this thoughtful kindness I set eyes in my earliest infancy on such prodigies of variety as Marie Lloyd, George Formby Senior, Maidie Scott, Harry Lauder and Little Tich; especially Little Tich, who for me will for ever be the funniest of all stage comedians.

Many years later, when I had become a London drama critic, my father would tease me for having fallen asleep at one of those early music-hall matinées. At the top of the bill, he said, was 'the greatest actress in the world', Sarah Bernhardt, playing the Lady of the Camellias in French. With some indignation I used always to deny this possibility, protesting, first, that Bernhardt could not possibly be playing in a mere music hall, and secondly, that I could not possibly fall asleep before such a performer, whatever my age.

But I have recently discovered that the dear man was absolutely right. Looking through old newspaper files I find that Sarah Bernhardt appeared at the top of a Glasgow Pavilion variety bill in the second week of November 1912 in the fifth act (the death scene) of that same play by Dumas *fils*. I was there, and I fell asleep! My old master, James Agate, would never have forgiven me for this, had I ever confessed it. For he was a great drama critic, and Bernhardt was his goddess. I was then not yet eight years old, and the incident may indicate that I was either already a good drama critic or already a bad one. Whatever it proves, the fact is incontrovertible that I once set eyes on Bernhardt—and was unable to keep them open!

I find that the *Glasgow Herald* dealt quite nobly with the visit: 'The average music-hall audiences seek the cheerful relaxation of comedy rather than the tonic sadness of tragedy, and the creation of a tragic atmosphere amid the whirl of a variety entertainment is a task that might daunt the most experienced actor. Indeed, last night, as one listened to the low sad music and the subdued murmur of conversation that preceded the appearance of Mme Bernhardt, one felt that one was awaiting the crucial point of some daring experiment. . . . But the genius of Mme Bernhardt, which renders the pathos of *La Dame aux Camélias* independent of language, makes the scene stand out from the various "turns" that precede it. . . . For Mme Bernhardt death is more than the cessation of life—it is the summing up of the pathos and the tragedy of earthly existence.' This seems to me not only fine, but positively agatian.

I had no great friends of my own age in childhood. In my first year or two at school the other children discovered that, though I was born in Ayrshire, both my parents were from the North of England (Westmorland and Yorkshire). I was dubbed in consequence 'a dirty Englishman', and resent such a term of abuse to this day. No less unpopular was my preferring to hug a Book instead of kicking or throwing or chasing or hitting a Ball all over the place. I hugged a one-volume Shakespeare before I could even read. It was an old edition, published by Messrs Dicks in The Strand, and had an illustrative engraving at the head of each play; although I lost my cherished copy in a school fire in 1919 I can remember still—and can clearly and easily recollect when trying to sleep in the dead of night—the illustration and caption for each play. Not only, for example, that Hamlet is saying 'Angels and ministers of grace defend us!' to the beckoning Ghost, but also that Beatrice is saying to Benedick, 'Against my will I am sent to bid you come to dinner', and that Titania is exclaiming on her first vision of Bottom with the ass's head, 'What angel wakes me from my flowery bed?' I can even, without strain, recollect the engraving and its caption of so unfamiliar a play as *King Henry VI: Part Three*. It is of the Duke of Gloster pointing his dripping sword down at the king's corpse and saying, 'Down, down to hell and say I sent thee thither!'

Never was there such an encouragement to read, and I was certainly learning to swim in Shakespeare by the age of eight or nine. Moreover, my inexhaustibly interesting father had seen Irving and Ellen Terry in *The Merchant of Venice* and *Olivia* (the dramatized *Vicar of Wakefield*). He had seen Irving by himself in *The Lyons Mail*, and a reputable touring actor called Osmund Tearle as Hamlet and Othello and other such heroes. And he would hold me spellbound with talk of these stage adventures even as Othello himself regaled that silly old man, Brabantio, who was Desdemona's dad. He would tell me, too, of the immense range of the theatre between Shakespeare, which I had yet to see, and vaudeville, in which I already revelled—of an actor called Wilson Barrett and of melodramas like *The Silver King*, and also of an audacious new playwright who was very much to my father's then somewhat Fabian mind. His name was Bernard Shaw.

As soon as I could read I learned by heart all those illustrative captions in my one-volume Shakespeare: 'It is the cause, it is the cause, my soul', said Othello; and 'How ill this taper burns—ha, who comes here?' said Brutus in his tent. I pored over 'Books for the Bairns', a series of digests of the classics, in brown paper covers and costing twopence each, as I remember. They were edited by W. T. Stead, who was another of my dad's 'great men'. Around the same time I pored over the newspaper column advertising the theatres in London (those in Glasgow, in the evening paper, were comparatively few and less exciting). And to this day, when I do research in the newspaper files and happen upon the years just before the First World War, it is no surprise to me to note—facts familiar to me since infancy—that there was a drama called *Drake* at His Majesty's in 1912; that Harry Pélissier's *Follies* were at the Apollo Theatre in the same year and had been appearing there annually for years and years before that; and that a Franz Lehár musical comedy, *The Count of Luxembourg*, put on at Daly's Theatre in 1911, was still running there early in 1912.

It was in this same year that three important happenings engaged my imagination—two of them important to the world at large and major 'sensations' in the news, the third exquisitely trivial and momentous only to me personally. The first was the sinking of the 'unsinkable' White Star liner *Titanic* on her maiden trip across the Atlantic. I clearly remember my father reading aloud a list of the celebrities who had perished, and pausing with awe at the name of his revered W. T. Stead, who had published not only the 'Books for the Bairns' but also a series of orange-coloured 'Penny Poets' which he himself was fond of collecting. The second happening was the death of Captain Scott and his brave team of Antarctic explorers. They were given up for lost early in the year and their bodies were not discovered until the end of it. And I clearly remember an enlightened schoolteacher reading us in class some pages of Captain Scott's last diary, culminating in the very simple and deeply moving (because very simple) last two sentences of all: 'We shall stick it out to the end, but we are getting weaker, of course, and the end cannot be far. It seems a pity but I do not think I can write any more.'

The third happening of the year 1912 was in my own little world of childish disappointment and delight. My family took a ten days' trip to London and decided that I was too young to be taken along with them; instead they foisted me upon kindly neighbours. They sent me postcards bought in the National Gallery and the Tate Gallery (a Van Dyck, a George Clausen). And they brought back for me a little toy cannon and—something upon which I pounced far more eagerly —the programme of *The Count of Luxembourg* which they had been to see in the pit at Daly's Theatre. In return they were plied with my questions. Where was Daly's? Where was Leicester Square? Was it near Covent Garden? Had they seen at least the outside of the Opera House? And of Drury Lane Theatre? And did they all 'go down The Strand', as the comedian Charles Whittle, in the best of his songs, was about that time suggesting that we all should do?

But most of all, and for many a long day, I pored over the Daly's Theatre programme. The very sound of the title of that musical comedy, *The Count of Luxembourg*, was to me as romantic as the perfume of Parma violets. The waltz tunes, which I heard my elders humming and my sister playing on the piano, were ineffably and lastingly pretty. At the age of seven I was already taking piano lessons, and a 'piano selection' from Franz Lehár's score was a very great incentive to attend to my music lessons. Time has not faded those dear three-four-time tunes. I am occasionally heard to strum them still, whether at home or in taverns, and I shall go to my grave thinking that the lilt of Franz Lehár and Oscar Straus and Leo Fall is much closer to my heart than all that jazz that followed later in the century.

I was learning to read letters as well as music notes simultaneously. Unhappily, I was considered to strum well enough when I was ten and to need no further music lessons. The result is that now—and in spite of a lifelong infatuation with music and a hopeless and unrequited passion for the pianoforte—I play no better than Wilde's Algernon, who says to his butler just after curtain-rise: 'I don't play accurately— anyone can play accurately—but I play with wonderful expression.' With wonderful ambition, too, when I am blissfully *tout seul*. Take Chopin alone. Not content with his mazurkas and valses and nocturnes (some of which almost anyone can play—badly) I tackle the rest of that great little master as well. Take the ballades, to mention nothing else. With wonderful expression I can play the opening of No 1 in G minor (six bars), the whole idyllic first page of No 2 in F (before the thunderstorm), *most* of the tender *first* page of No 3 in A flat, and of No 4 in F minor at least the five serene and celestial chords (before the infernal deluge of the last two pages). What I do with all the other music of the ballades in particular and of Chopin in general is very much my own business!

In the early spring of 1914 I saw my first Peter Pan (the delectable

Pauline Chase), and I discovered thirty years later that the name of the nice cheeky little boy playing Slightly was Master Noël Coward. (It was his only appearance in *Peter Pan*, which he calls 'the Mecca of all child actors', and he is characteristically funny about the experience in his autobiographical *Present Indicative*.) A few weeks before this I had seen the pantomime at Glasgow's Theatre Royal—as I successfully clamoured to do in each and all of those years. It was *Old King Cole*, and the Principal Boy (called Clara Beck) sang to the Principal Girl (called Ivey Latimer) an ineffably beautiful song called 'If I Should Plant a Tiny Seed in the Garden of your Heart', in which I am note-perfect and word-perfect (at least as to the refrain) to this day.

With a curious vividness I remember also, about this pantomime, that the large and jolly comedian John Humphries greeted somebody or other—it may have been one of the Brothers Egbert—with the uproariously received remark, 'What a beautiful suit of Mallaby-Deeleys!' Hating then, as now, to miss a joke I begged my father, even before we got home, to tell me the point of this. The point was that Mallaby Deeley was a current and celebrated millionaire who had made some of his millions on men's clothing—cheap tailoring on mass-production lines. At that time, it seemed, his name was very much in the news—more than ever before, in fact—because he had just spent at least two of his much-talked-about millions in buying a great chunk of central London, the Covent Garden district, from Herbrand, eleventh Duke of Bedford, in whose family it had been for centuries.

Now does the patient reader see to what all this autobiographical matter has ingeniously led? The whole of the Duke of Bedford's Covent Garden Estate had been bought by Mr H. Mallaby Deeley, M.P. for the Harrow Division, in December 1913, and this magnificent business deal was still in the news. The price had not been disclosed at the time, but it was said to run—very vaguely—into 'millions', and represented one of the largest if not *the* largest purchase of real property ever to take place in this country. Mallaby Deeley stated at the time that he was not associated with others in the purchase and that the negotiations had all been conducted on his behalf alone.

The property occupied one of the most valuable sites in central London, and the streets and buildings which it comprised were steeped in historical and theatrical associations. Among the well-known public buildings forming part of the estate were the Royal Opera House,

Drury Lane Theatre, Covent Garden Market, the Aldwych Theatre, the Strand Theatre, the Waldorf Hotel, Bow Street Police Court, and the National Sporting Club.

The estate was freehold and extended to some nineteen acres. It lay, roughly speaking, between The Strand and Long Acre on the south and north, and Aldwych and St Martin's Lane on the east and west, although the whole of the land within these limits was not included in the property. Twenty-six streets, or parts of streets, were on the estate; but in the case of some of them—for example, in Long Acre and Bow Street—only one or two private houses actually belonged to it. The names of the streets were Aldwych, Bedford Court, Bedford Street, Bow Street, Broad Court, Burleigh Street, Catherine Street, Chandos Street, Cross Court, Crown Court, Drury Lane, Exeter Street, Floral Street, Garrick Street, Henrietta Street, James Street, King Street, Long Acre, Maiden Lane, Martlett Court, New Street, Russell Street, Southampton Street, Tavistock Street, Wellington Street, York Street.

Mallaby Deeley made it perfectly plain in an interview in *The Times*—a journalistic feature, by the way, which was said to have been invented by the recently drowned W. T. Stead—that this had been an entirely private transaction between himself and the Duke of Bedford. He stated: 'There is very little to say about the future. I have no intentions. I have bought the estate purely as a private investment and the estate will be carried on just as it has been hitherto. It will certainly not be turned into a company, and there is no part of it that will be turned into a company.' Mark his words!

Those negotiations had been in progress since the previous September, and the agreement was signed three weeks before the news was published. The Duke of Bedford had surrendered the whole of his interest in the estates; even his freehold box at the Royal Opera House, said to be the finest in the whole building, as well as the freehold boxes at Drury Lane, the Strand and the Aldwych Theatres, passed to the purchaser as part of the conveyance. Mr Mallaby Deeley repeated to the interviewer that he was unwilling to disclose the price paid for the estate. He was aware of the extraordinary public interest which had been excited by the purchase, but when he made his offer the extraordinary nature of the transaction had not occurred to him. It was only when he first saw the plan that he recognized its magnitude. 'But,' he added, 'I have carried through the purchase and the financial part of the transaction, and I have not had a sleepless night.' Lucky non-insomniac Mallaby Deeley! He was then reminded that there was much speculation concerning the price he had paid, but he once more declined to satisfy public curiosity on the point: 'It is, of course, evident that the value of the estate is enormous. Twenty-six streets and, besides several famous theatres, there are two important banks and the Tavistock, the Bedford and the Covent Garden Hotels, besides other very valuable property.'

Possibly I should forbear comment on matters which are beyond my understanding. But let me say only that this soundly sleeping master financier strikes me as an odd mixture of a naïve little boy and a big businessman of the most alarming order, and that I am irresistibly reminded of the ironic title of a music-hall sketch toured around this time by a comedian called Bert Coote. It was called *A Lamb on Wall Street*.

At the conclusion of the interview Mallaby Deeley was asked how the negotiations with the Duke of Bedford were begun, and he replied that the estate was offered to him directly. He made an offer which was refused. He then made a second offer which was accepted. He explained that he had been interested in land and houses since he was a small boy, and he knew perfectly the value of the estate. Offers of estates were frequently made to him. Among them was the site of St George's Hospital, which again was entirely a private transaction. The statement which had gained currency that he intended to erect a large hotel on the site was quite inaccurate. He never had any such intention. If a hotel was erected it would be done by a syndicate to whom the land would be leased.

Invited to express his opinion as to the probable effect of the Government's urban land proposals upon the value of land in London, this financier said: 'I have no fear that any future legislation can depreciate the value of property in London. No legislation can prevent a landlord and his tenant coming to a fair agreement. I have considered Mr Lloyd George's proposals very carefully and I have not the slightest fear of the effect of his proposed legislation on either rural or urban land. So long as the legislation proposed is not downright confiscation it does not alarm me in the least.'

Nearly a whole page of *The Times* for 17th December 1913 was devoted to this vast transaction. One full column speculated on the price paid, just as all its readers appeared to be speculating with wideawake inquisitiveness. Any attempt at a computation of the price, apart from any special terms which might have been arranged between vendor and purchaser, was complicated by the question of the value of the market tolls. Whenever in recent years it had been possible for vendors of property to append the words 'toll free' to the description of freeholds in the neighbourhood of Covent Garden satisfactory sales had invariably resulted.

It was understood that the Duke of Bedford had acquired in recent years many of the properties which had been offered for sale in this same area. Estimates of the value of exemption from tolls varied with different valuers. Anyhow 'the capitalization of the tolls introduces an element which makes comparison with other properties in the neighbourhood of little or no use as a means of estimating the probable amount of the purchase money'.

Finally there is a comment on the Duke himself and on his Grace's policy and practice: 'The Duke of Bedford was one of the pioneers in the process known as the "breaking-up of estates", by which hundreds of thousands of acres of agricultural land have changed hands, and if his example in regard to urban properties is to be followed by other great ground-landlords in London, especially if they offer the tenants the first opportunity of acquiring premises, the ownership map of London will be altered out of recognition, and, incidentally, the public will be able to gauge the extent and reality of complaints which are now made on behalf of town tenants.'

On this same occasion the Duke of Bedford was the subject of a brief biographical sketch, and was particularly praised for his generosity in having recently presented a young pigmy hippopotamus to the London Zoological Society, of which since 1889 he had been president: 'Although his disposition is to prefer a private life, the Duke has not held aloof from the public duties which naturally fall to the lot of a great nobleman.' Thus he was Lord Lieutenant of Middlesex, and president of the Middlesex Territorial Force Association, chairman of the Bedfordshire County Council, and held other lofty sinecures. More actively he was a J.P. and D.L. for that same county, and had filled the office of first Mayor of Holborn in 1900.

But what of Mallaby Deeley's biography until that date, when he was exactly fifty years old? There seems to be a good deal between the lines of the sketch. Educated at Shrewsbury and Trinity College,

Cambridge, he took an honours degree in law in 1885, was called to the Bar by the Inner Temple, but never practised. He stood for Parliament in 1910 and became Unionist Member for Harrow, but we read that his voice was very rarely heard in the House. He played golf at Mitcham but would appear to have been more interested in purchasing property, including golf courses galore. But let *The Times* itself speak, with its customary discretion:

'This is by no means the first large deal in property in which Mr Mallaby Deeley has been concerned, although it greatly exceeds in magnitude all his previous transactions of the kind. Besides being the owner of a number of golf courses he has within the last few years acquired a number of important properties in London on which hotels or residential buildings are erected or about to be erected. He first came into considerable prominence in 1909, when he was at the head of the syndicate which bought the Piccadilly Hotel. The price was said to be £500,000. He was also the purchaser of St James's Court, a large block of flats in Buckinghamgate. The price paid on this occasion was £250,000.

'In the early summer of this year he was again concerned in two large projects which excited a great amount of public interest. The first was the Northern Junction Railway Bill, of which he was the principal promoter. The Parliamentary struggle over this measure will be well remembered, for it encountered a storm of opposition owing to the way in which the proposed line of railway would have interfered with the amenities of the Hampstead Garden Suburb. This scheme involved a capital of £2,000,000, and in the course of the proceedings before the Parliamentary Select Committee Mr Mallaby Deeley pledged himself to find the capital required. The opposition, however, was too strong for him, and although the proposal was supported by the War Office, the Bill was rejected. Not the least interesting aspect of this project was that the most formidable opposition came from Mr Mallaby Deeley's own constituents in the Hampstead Garden Suburb and other places which lie in the Harrow Division.

'The other important scheme with which he was connected this year was the purchase of the site of St George's Hospital, for which he gave £460,000.

'The realization of a large urban estate in the way in which the present transaction has been carried out is without precedent in the annals of London real estate. Large areas at Kensington and in Islington and elsewhere, including a Greenwich estate, have been offered owing to death or for other reasons, but no such large and compact area in Central London has been dealt with.'

When Mallaby-Deeley (now Sir Harry, and hyphenated) eventually died at his château near Cannes—for the sound as well as the unsound sleeper must eventually die—*The Times* was just a shade less guarded. This was in February 1937:

'He was noteworthy among a half-dozen or so of daring dealers in real estate who were prominent a quarter of a century ago for his insistence on direct personal negotiation with the principals in property matters. He seemed never to need detailed professional valuations and minute legal or other investigations in his transactions. When the idea of acquiring any particular property had occurred to him he would follow it up by an interview with the owner, and usually, if the latter had the least intention of disposing of his interest, Mallaby-Deeley would come from the meeting place with a half-sheet of notepaper recording the proposed contract. It was in this way that he settled the purchase of Covent Garden with the Duke of Bedford for just over £1,750,000.'

And again:

'He had a remarkable quality of foresight in estate matters, and his judgment in such matters as the future of Covent Garden was rarely found to be at fault. As he remarked in 1913, when buying Covent Garden, there would be no changes and there was no syndicate. Part of his success in real estate ventures was due doubtless to that individual freedom of choice and action. The smallest and most efficient of committees must involve delay compared to the decisive activating of a single mind. The buying of the site of St George's Hospital for £460,000 was one of his most talked-of achievements.'

And finally the first mention in *The Times* of what the comedians of the day were calling 'Mallaby-Deeleys':

'To many of the general public, however, he was best known as the promoter of a scheme for the retailing of ready-made clothes

at a low price. This venture in tailoring reflected his lifelong love
of being himself faultlessly dressed and of seeing others enabled to
dress well. He was never heard to regret that, so far from yielding
a profit, the tailoring scheme put him out of pocket by about
£60,000.'

Researching into the past it never does to ignore the *Guardian* (that
used to be the *Manchester Guardian*), and it is no surprise at all to find
that in 1913 that journal dealt more racily than anybody else with
what was 'going on' about Covent Garden. The writer quoted is—or
was for nearly a century—'Private Wire', the London column being
headed 'Our London Letter—by Private Wire', the reference, of
course, being to the fact that most of the column came up from London
overnight to be printed in Manchester. 'What does Private Wire say
about it?' was a question regularly heard in Fleet Street among coveys
of journalists, and no humble soldier—he was really half-a-dozen
unsigned writers at least—was ever so pithy, lively and literate!

The quotations here following are from the pen of the London
editor, James Bone, who wrote the celebrated *London Perambulator*.
There is no means of proving this fact, but I would willingly swear
to recognizing his flavour and his tang: he was my London editor on
the M.G. for eight years and my good friend for twenty-five. The
first paragraph is headed 'The Big Deal' and it begins very characteristically and with a delightful allusiveness:

'Major Booth Voysey in Mr Granville Barker's play *The Voysey
Inheritance*, when he heard of his father's defalcations, was staggered
like the rest of the family, but when he hears it is for a hundred
thousand pounds his breast swells, he strokes his moustache, he
straddles, and says, "Quite a big thing—what!" That was how
London heard today of the sale of the whole Covent Garden
area by the Duke of Bedford to Mr Mallaby Deeley. At first it
seemed almost a disgrace that an ancient ducal estate should pass
out of the family, and then when we heard the sum of five millions
whispered as the purchase price everyone felt that it was "quite a
big thing", and London was a great place for a man to be in.

'This is the second startler that Mr Mallaby Deeley has given us.
The first was, of course, the news that he had purchased the site
of St George's Hospital at Hyde Park Corner for about half a
million. It has been stated that he is acting alone in the Covent

Garden purchase, but in carrying out a transfer of this magnitude it is safe to say that not even the greatest magnates in England with family accumulations could act alone.

'The question everyone is asking is what schemes lie behind the purchase. A belief in the Market itself is that it includes big extensions, probably involving the pulling down of the old building on the north side and a rebuilding of a large part of the district for fruit and vegetable salesmen's showrooms and offices. It is thought that the development will lie in that way and not in the way of big new hotels and blocks of flats.'

'Private Wire' returns to the subject two days later. He is obviously on fire with it, and he has no less obviously been in the Market itself asking the tradesmen, the salesmen and the porters all about it:

'Speculations are rife. What will Mr Mallaby Deeley do with it? The fact that it lies between the Shaftesbury Avenue improvement and the Kingsway improvement means that its value will steadily increase. He is, in fact, willing to sell to the London County Council if it will pay enough. . . . As to the actual financial arrangements of the transaction two rumours are abroad. One is that the Duke has only changed from owner to mortgagor, and the other connects the Norwich Union Insurance Company with the deal, probably for no other reason than Mr Mallaby Deeley's connection with that institution.'

Note how this great journalist disseminates more rumours without either denying them or confirming them. He was interested—and makes us interested—in what might happen as well as in what had happened. He had unending curiosity in motive and incentive as well as in deeds and dealings, in what might happen as well as in what had happened, in eventualities as well as in events. He liked to get the news from the lips of the individuals who were making it. He had an unslakeable desire to know also what the mere spectator was thinking about it all. I have seen him often—with a joke at the end of his tongue and never too seriously—asking a newspaper-seller in Fleet Street what he made of the news, or inquiring of a railway porter or a market porter for his angle on what might be afoot. He got his information, too, without incurring any resentment or temper, greatly helped by his own affability. They knew that this square-headed old codger was not 'the Law' whatever else he might be. Once, when we were walking together in The Strand and he had just asked a newsboy some question or other, I said I should one day try to describe his insatiable curiosity about life in general, and he replied with his characteristic chuckle: 'No, just call me inquisitive. That's the word—inquisitive.' But it was more than that.

What happened next struck 'Private Wire' dumb for quite a time. It was nothing less than the sale of Covent Garden Estate by Mr Mallaby Deeley to no more unexpected a person than Sir Joseph Beecham (father of the then Mr Thomas Beecham). This happened in June 1914, exactly six months after the Big Deal. In March there had been the annual dinner of the Wholesale Fruit and Potato Trade's Benevolent Society, at which Mr Mallaby Deeley himself presided.

He vehemently denied the rumour—only one of many such rumours before and since—that the Market was going to remove itself to a more convenient part of London. *The Times* reported his speech: 'A Mr Percy Harris had recently talked quite glibly—in *The Times* itself—about the pending removal of Covent Garden. But nobody wanted the removal of the Market. The traders themselves were certainly not anxious for a change. It had been said that Covent Garden was not centrally situated. In his opinion for its purpose it could not be more centrally situated. The question of the holding up of traffic was a small one, as every businessman knew. No main thoroughfare passed through the Market, and therefore exceedingly little inconvenience was caused by it.' So 'twas said.

A little later during the same function Mr Mallaby Deeley replied to the toast of his health and opined that the Market, far from moving itself, would greatly expand and improve: 'I hope and believe that the salesmen will in the future have reason for knowing that they will be more firmly secured in their tenancies and their businesses, and will, in addition, have greater security in possessing—what they do not possess now—a most valuable asset, namely good will. . . . That asset of security will be given as far as it is possible to give it under the charter.'

Three months after this speech the stunning news leaked out that Sir Joseph Beecham was negotiating to buy the entire district. He had had two successful seasons of grand opera at Drury Lane Theatre in which his son (then in his early thirties) was principal conductor. In the high summer of this negotiation there had been a markedly successful season of Russian opera—works of Moussorgsky, Borodin, Rimsky-Korsakov, which were then quite new to London.

'Private Wire' now indulges in elaborate speculations and surmises as to what Sir Joseph may be 'up to'. Is he 'out' to be a property magnate, or to build a new and permanent opera house, or both? Anyhow, he goes on:

'It is unthinkable that after so successful a season as the present one (all previous box-office takings have been surpassed again and again this year), Sir Joseph should be content to rest with folded hands while others [meaning the Royal Opera Syndicate] take advantage of the great popularity of opera at the present moment—a popularity which Sir Joseph himself has been mainly instrumental in creating. The difficulty, however, begins when one starts to speculate as to what the next development might be. Sir Joseph has shown himself as enterprising as he is discriminating in the selection of operas. He gave us first Richard Strauss operas, then the Russian ballet, and finally Russian operas. If he intends to go yet further there is apparently only one direction in which to advance—namely, to establish once and for all permanent opera in London. The project seems at first almost too daring for anyone to venture on it. But so far, at any rate, the public has kept pace with the step made towards this final goal. This year we have had, on the whole, as much opera as most "permanent" houses on the Continent. The time seems certainly opportune for a manager who, like Sir Joseph, combines business capacity with an artistic conscience.'

My comment on this interesting note would be that it seems likely that Sir Joseph had far more of the capacity than the conscience, just as his celebrated son had more of the conscience and far less of the capacity. Sir Joseph, a very remarkable man who deserves a biography to himself and has never had one, seems sedulously to have developed in himself a fine taste for all the fine arts, and yet seems to have had hardly anything that could be called fine taste when he was a young man.

We shall see this when we read and reproduce his obituaries. Here I am not being at all premature, or looking too far ahead too early. As big a sensation as any other in those sensational years was his very sudden death in October 1916. In July 1914 there had been a statement in *The Times* about the intensely complicated position. I make no apology for reproducing this statement and so much else on this subject which seems to me permanently fascinating and character-revealing in a quite subtle way. Any attempt of my own to disentangle these knots would only entangle them further:

'The negotiations for the re-sale of the Covent Garden estate, it was announced yesterday, have been brought to a successful issue, and a contract has been signed. The purchaser is Sir Joseph Beecham, but when the negotiations first came to light Sir Joseph confessed that he was not the only one interested, and it was stated for the first time yesterday that with him "is associated" Mr Alexander Lawson Ormrod, of Messrs Lawson and Ormrod, stock-brokers, of Manchester.

'The vendor, so far as can be gathered from the statements issued by the solicitors to the parties, is technically the Duke of Bedford himself. Mr Mallaby Deeley, according to the statement of the purchaser's solicitor, is an "assenting party". According to the statement of his own solicitors, it is he who has accepted Sir Joseph Beecham's offer, and £75,000 already paid on deposit has "been received by him".

'The explanation of the apparent discrepancy no doubt is this. Mr Mallaby Deeley struck a bargain over the estate with the Duke of Bedford last November, but that bargain, his solicitors now explain, has not, on account of a dispute over boundaries, been completely carried out. It is, therefore, to be assumed that the Duke of Bedford still holds the title deeds, and must appear as vendor in any re-sale of the property, though the purchase money is taken by Mr Mallaby Deeley.'

Sir Joseph Beecham was found dead in his bed at his Hampstead residence on the morning of 23rd October 1916. Sir Thomas, his son, did not appear to be either proud of or embarrassed by the dusty, sulphur-yellow, laxative pills on which the family's fortunes were founded. Sir Thomas simply never mentioned them. But Sir Joseph had no such *mauvaise honte*. The pills had been the invention of Sir Thomas's grandfather, another Thomas, a humble chemist of St Helens, Lancashire; and on Sir Joseph's death an old resident of St Helens wrote to the newspapers to say that he clearly remembered when the pill business was in its infancy, seeing its founder, Thomas Beecham, offering his wares for sale in the market-place of that town. It was while he frequented the market-place that a woman one day interrupted his speech by shouting out that his pills were 'worth a guinea a box', and he at once replied that he would put that phrase on every box he produced in future. He did so.

Sir Joseph was no less proud of the same phrase that made his pills a public demand. When he was still a young man he issued a penny musical magazine—it was called the *Beecham Portfolio*—in which ballads and piano pieces were interspersed with this same advertisement, at a period when his gifted son was not old enough to teach him better taste. I used to possess two issues of this magazine in my own infancy when learning to play the piano, and I first met one or two of Mendelssohn's *Songs without Words* in them—Victorian romanticism at its best and worst! Another issue came into my possession only the other day and quite by chance. It is a cluster of ballads both sentimental and jovial—ballads like Balfe's *In This Old Chair My Father Sat* and ditties like *Here's a Health unto His Majesty* ('as sung by Mr. Santley')—which never did any harm to anybody. There are a very few piano pieces also, like *Stéphanie Gavotte* by the otherwise unremembered Czibulka. And then there is an especially composed *morceau* called *The Guinea Pills Gavotte*!

And whenever a ballad does not quite fill out the page there is one of these advertisements of which a typical example runs: 'JARS in the family are more often the result of DISORDERED DIGESTION than most people know. BEECHAM'S PILLS will keep peace in a family by curing Sick Headache, Weak Stomach etc. etc. etc. and all Bilious and Nervous Disorders arising from these causes. WORTH A GUINEA A BOX.' This, of course, was twenty years before the Grand Opera Seasons, and it would surprise me very greatly to learn that any such advertisement appeared in the Drury Lane programmes for those triumphant seasons that led up to the very verge of the First World War.

My dear old James Bone of the *Guardian* had the advantage of knowing Sir Joseph Beecham personally, and on the pharmaceutical musician's death he had—writing again under the guise of 'Private Wire'—his own gentle brand of frank and amusing revelations to offer:

'Though one of the greatest advertisers of the time, Sir Joseph Beecham preferred to keep himself out of the limelight, as he truly told the Royal Commission on Advertisements some time ago. Though he had a house in London and stayed there some days every week, he was totally unknown to the vast majority of Londoners till the public musical activities of his son, Sir Thomas, directed attention to him. In the last few years he was a familiar figure at the opera, especially during the performances of the famous Russians.

'He was himself in his youth more than a fair organist, and was a shrewd judge of music. He was typical of all that is best in the North-country industrial magnate. I remember that once he purposely shocked a very superior young musical amateur, who was rhapsodising with futile superlatives about the Russian opera, by saying that in music, as in everything else, the thing is "to deliver the goods".

'Another typical remark of his was when a musician kept him waiting for an appointment. He said: "I have never been late for an appointment in my life, even when it was with an office boy to sack him." He was very methodical in small things. On the Underground he did not take a ticket, but travelled without one in virtue of the railway director's golden key which he carried.

'Sir Joseph Beecham was an extensive picture collector of nineteenth-century English pictures. So far as I recollect he had a dozen of Turner's late Italian water colours, and his chief treasure was Turner's famous picture of the St. Gothard diligence overturned in the snow. My impression of his oil pictures was that the quality varied sharply, and that while a number of his Constables and masters of the Norwich School would do credit to any collection, many of the others would have been weeded out by a careful collector. I remarked to him that he seemed to have come through many stages in his art interest, and in his reply he told me how he began to collect.

'He said, with a frankness that characterized all his doings, that the first picture he bought was a plate issued by a sporting paper of the redoubtable Tom Sayers, who met Heenan in the famous fight in 1860. He was a boy then, very keen about boxing. He had it framed and hung in his bedroom, and he added to it plates of other fistic champions. His art interests enlarged, and by and by he gave up sporting plates and collected pictures.'

To whom does this whole congeries of property—and most especially Covent Garden Market itself—nowadays belong? I have vainly been trying to find out for years; and in recent months I have asked a great variety of the Market's functionaries, beadles, wardens, overseers, merchants, salesmen and porters; and have received a great variety of answers usually delivered without the slightest hesitancy. It belongs, it would seem, to the Queen, to the Crown, to the Government, to Vested Interests, to Covent Garden Properties, Ltd. It belongs to the ages. It belongs to me.

CHAPTER TWO

THE PIAZZA – CABBAGES AND KINGS

The Piazza or Great Square is the topographical centre and secular heart of Covent Garden—just as St Paul's Church, adjoining it on the west side, is the sacred heart of the district. Why the Great Square from the start was called the Piazza—and still is, occasionally—and what exactly is a Piazza, are debatable points which ought to be cleared up at the outset. If they can be!

Piazza is simply the Italian for a town-square just as *place* is the French, *plaza* the Spanish, and *platz* the German. Inigo Jones and the Earl of Bedford between them seem to have devised the non-English-sounding name of Piazza for their central square because it was modelled on the piazza in Livorno or Leghorn, and this in turn seems to have suggested the Place des Vosges in Paris. In both the Italian and French town-squares the borders of the rectangle are arcaded. From the very start the Covent Garden square was arcaded (Pl. 4) on three sides only, the south side being taken up with the Earl of Bedford's garden. From the very start, also, the word piazza was used indiscriminately in the singular and the plural, and it was used also to signify arcade or arcades as well as square. The Danish authority on London architecture, S. E. Rasmussen, says as much very succinctly: '... The arcades were so popular that the foreign word *Piazza* soon became synonymous with the arcades instead of with the square.' It is of little avail for the *Shorter Oxford Dictionary* to say that this use of the word is 'erroneous'. What is done is done, be it wrong or right. And from the beginning and in all sorts of context the word piazza or piazzas is used to mean the square, or the arcades round the square, or the houses in the arcades round the square.

The Dictionary itself quotes an extremely early example of this use (or misuse) giving the date, 1695, but not the author: 'They live in one of the Piazzas in Covent Garden.' Samuel Pepys later in the same century is continually visiting the Piazza or the Piazzas, for either good or bad company. His various uses and connotations of the word in both the singular and the plural are recommended to any student in search of a profitable subject for a thesis. Sometimes he is clearly visiting one of the great and rich houses, uniformly built, on the edge of the Piazza proper. Sometimes he is, no less clearly, poking about the bagnios in the side-streets skirting the Piazza proper. Sometimes he would appear to be waiting unavailingly in the middle of the Great Square, as in the entry for 9th April 1667 with its coy Latin *sed* for *but*, its discreet Italian *visti ensemble* for *seen together*, and its cautious French *baiser* for *kiss*:

'So home to dinner, and after dinner I took coach and to the King's house, and by and by comes after me my wife with W. Hewer and his mother and Barker, and there we saw *The Tameing of a Shrew* [Shakespeare's play as altered by the comedian John Lacy] which has some very good pieces in it, but generally is but a mean play; and the best part, Sawny [the hero's Scottish servant rendered with north-country accent] done by Lacy, hath not half its life, by reason of the words, I suppose, not being understood, at least by me. After the play was done, as I came so I went away alone, and had a mind to have taken out Knip [his play-actress-cum-mistress] to have taken the ayre with her, and to that end sent a porter in to her that she should take a coach and come to me to the Piazza in Covent Garden, where I waited for her but was doubtful I might have done ill in doing it if we should be visti ensemble, sed elle was gone out, and so I was eased of my care, and therefore away to Westminster to the Swan, and therefore did baiser le little missa. . . .' [And here intrude the three dots of editor Wheatley in one of his exasperating attacks of pudicity.]

Lord Byron considered Inigo Jones's attempt to import the word Piazza 'an affectation', which is somewhat rich on the part of a writer whom one is often tempted to dismiss as being affectation incarnate. But James Bone, in his superb book, *The London Perambulator*, is altogether more quotable and more sound, not only on the word Piazza, but also on the institution and infiltration of the Square in general:

'Inigo Jones took the idea from the Italian piazzas when he designed the first London square (and in a John-Bullish way we have attached the word piazza, not to the parallelogram of Covent Garden, but to the arcaded side that still remains), but he produced something quite different in the residential square with a common garden in the centre. The nobles moved to Lincoln's Inn Fields, St. James's Square, Berkeley Square, and Soho Square from their riverside mansions secluded in private grounds, and began to live in a house that was only one of a row of similar houses, each owned by an equal and immediately in contact with public opinion. It must have opened a new life to the early settlers—and especially to their children—in the Stuart squares; and from then on the squares must have had a social significance in the disposition of upper and middle class London life. The square also maintained a standard of architecture and amenities that gave way too often to muddle and pretentiousness when the aristocratic landowners ceased to lay out and build, or parted with their ground. They had given the work to their own architects, who were men of repute, maintaining a level of taste throughout the design even in its humblest details, whereas the newer developers of suburbs were usually content to do without an architect at all. So Bloomsbury remains today with an unpretentious urbane charm of good proportions, and shy hints of elegance in fanlights and balconies.'

It can be gathered from all these considerations, both historical and architectural, that Covent Garden Market—when finally it moves from its present position—had no business to be there at all, or to have been there for three hundred years and more. It began with a mere market stall or two within or alongside the Earl of Bedford's garden on the south side of the Piazza (Pl. 3).

Through the years and even the centuries the marketing business came to fill the entire square and the arcades surrounding it, and then oversprawled into James Street and Long Acre, Russell Street and Bow Street, Tavistock Street almost to The Strand, into Southampton Street, along Maiden Lane and Henrietta Street and King Street. The two great theatres—the Royal Opera House and Drury Lane—are two islands of culture in this uncouth and tempestuous sea of vegetables, flowers and fruit. (Other cultural havens are, of course, the various warehouses, offices and showrooms of publishers.)

The contrast is marvellously dramatic, an unending source of wonder and pleasure to those, like myself, who love the wildest possible contrast between the couth and uncouth, the rich and the poor, the articulate and the hesitant, the polished and the rugged. With a mixture of diabolical cunning and the instinct of genius, Bernard Shaw chose the portico of St Paul's Church in the dead middle of Covent Garden market for the first act of his comedy of class distinctions, *Pygmalion*. His introduction to the act in the printed text of the play runs thus: 'Covent Garden at 11.15 p.m. Torrents of heavy summer rain. Pedestrians running for shelter into the market and under the portico of St Paul's Church, where there are already several people, among them a lady and her daughter in evening dress [fresh from the Opera]. They are all peering out gloomily at the rain, except one man with his back to the rest [Professor Higgins] who seems wholly preoccupied with a notebook in which he is writing busily.' He is, of course, making notes about the Cockney vowels and consonants of the grubby flower girl, Eliza Doolittle, who is trying to sell her violets to these sheltering toffs. The introduction to the immensely successful musical version, *My Fair Lady*, is slightly different in wording but exactly the same in effect: 'Outside the Royal Opera House, Covent Garden, Time: After-theatre, a cold March night. At rise of curtain the opera is just over. Richly gowned, beautifully tailored Londoners are pouring from the Opera House and making their way across Covent Garden in search of taxis. Some huddle together under the columns of St Paul's Church which are partially in view on one side of the stage. On the opposite side, there is a smudge-pot fire around which a quartet of costermongers are warming themselves. Calls of "Taxi" punctuate the icy air.' The description of the flower girl Eliza is very much that of Shaw with a few modifications: 'She wears a little sailor hat of black straw that has long been exposed to the dust and soot of London and has seldom if ever been brushed. Her hair needs washing rather badly; its mousy colour can hardly be natural. She wears a shoddy shawl, a dirty blouse with a coarse apron. Her boots are much the worse for wear. She is no doubt as clean as she can afford to be, but compared to the ladies she is very dirty. . . .'

It is very odd that extremely few of the most modern guides to London draw attention to this remarkable fact—that one of the best-known plays in the whole wide world and the most wide-spreading musical, not to mention the film of the musical, should have its opening scene set under the portico of St Paul's Church in the middle of the world's most celebrated fruit market. It is almost the first thing I point out to any overseas visitor who comes my way, especially the American sort. Among these have been one of the best practising drama critics, Walter Kerr, and his witty playwriting wife, Jean Kerr. They were appreciative. I seem to remember this couple lunching with me at Rules, and eventually penetrating to my attic in King Street where the witty wife, ignoring my books and treasures, took in my heaps of accumulated newspapers at one glance and remarked: 'I see you have the occupational malady of most journalists— *piles*!'

The two most celebrated painters at the Court of Charles II, Sir Peter Lely and Sir Godfrey Kneller, had their studios in the Piazza, a clear proof if any were wanted that this first of all our squares was then highly fashionable. Lely (1618–80), a Dutchman by blood and birth, came over to England in the train of Prince William of Orange when the latter married Mary, daughter of Charles I. He painted both several times. I have also seen his portrait of Oliver Cromwell, rather surprisingly in the Pitti Palace at Florence. On the Restoration the new king Charles II is said to have restored Lely to favour, though he seems never really to have been out of favour. Pepys often visited his studio during his long heyday. Thus in June 1662 he writes: 'I walked to Lilly, the painter's, where I saw, among other rare things, the Duchesse of York, her whole body, sitting in state in a chair, in white satin . . .'

In October of the same year, 1662, Pepys again visited Lely's studio, this time finding him at home: 'With Commissioner Pett to Mr Lilly's, the great painter, who came forth to us; but believing that I came to bespeak a picture, he prevented it by telling us he should not be at leisure these three weeks, which methinks is a rare thing. And then to see in what pomp his table was laid for himself to go to dinner; and here, among other pictures, saw the so much desired by me picture of Lady Castlemaine, which is a most blessed picture; and one that I must have a copy of.' Later and elsewhere Pepys describes Lely as 'a mighty proud man' and 'full of state'. He kept his pride and state to the end when he was buried by torchlight in St Paul's Church round the corner. And indeed for many years as a painter he had no serious rival until the coming of Kneller in 1678.

Godfrey Kneller (1646–1723) came from Lübeck in North Germany and was the portrait-painting son of a portrait-painter. While still touring Europe as a student he came to London at the invitation of Jonathan Banks, a Hamburg merchant there. His portraits of Banks and his family attracted the admiration of Mr Vernon, secretary to the Duke of Monmouth, who told the Duke about the German prodigy, and the Duke in turn told the King. The last had just commissioned a portrait from Sir Peter Lely at the request of James, Duke of York. Monmouth obtained leave for Kneller to draw the king's portrait at the same sitting. This took place in the presence of the two royal dukes and other members of the Court, and at the end of the sitting Kneller had not only nearly completed the portrait (he seems to have been a much faster worker than Lely) but had also obtained so good a likeness as to excite the wonder of all present. Wonderment was expressed not only by the King but by Lely himself. What a subject for a painting by a Pettie or an Orchardson, if today we had a Pettie or even an Orchardson! Kneller's future was assured on account of this single session. Being still only thirty-two and exceptionally good-looking, with a graceful figure and a confident manner, Kneller found commissions pouring in upon him. He moved house from Durham Yard, on the south side of The Strand, to a larger house in the Piazza at Covent Garden, where he continued to reside and practise for twenty-one years.

Lely's paint has lasted better than Kneller's, but the latter would seem to have been a more engaging and less arrogant man. Or let us say that he was more witty in his own conceit. Pope once said to him: 'Sir Godfrey, I believe if the Almighty had had your assistance, the world would have been made more perfect'. And the artist, laying his hand upon the poet's shoulder, answered him: ''Fore God, sir, I believe so'. Better still was his remark to the Bishop of Rochester that the following were his articles of religion: 'That God loved all ingenious persons; that painting was the most ingenious of all arts; and that he himself was the most ingenious of all painters.'

Sir Godfrey Kneller's house in the Piazza was on the site of the western side of what is now the Floral Hall or chief flower market. It is described in an advertisement dated 1714 as having 'a front room 42 ft by 19 ft and 12 ft high, with a garden attached to the mansion

150 ft by 40 ft', and if these measurements are accurate the Kneller menage occupied quite a slab of the Piazza itself. Ten reigning sovereigns sat to Kneller for their portraits, and he came to outdo even Sir Peter Lely in splendour and popularity. In 1703 he purchased and moved into a house in Great Queen Street near Lincoln's Inn Fields. He also had an extensive country estate at Whitton, near Twickenham. This, much altered, is now Kneller Hall and has long been used as the Royal School of Military Music. With a mixture of good luck and strategy I recently succeeded in spending a night therein hoping to see Sir Godfrey Kneller's ghost. But I have since discovered that, though buried in the garden there, he did not die there. He died instead in his house in Great Queen Street whence his body was borne to Kneller Hall for burial. Possibly for this reason my sleep was undisturbed except for a romantic and welcome bugle-call at sunrise.

Kneller's house in the Piazza was eventually taken by that prince of ceiling painters, Sir James Thornhill, whose work one still admires in the great dining-hall of the Royal Naval College at Greenwich, and also at Windsor and Hampton Court, where his patron was Queen Anne. He was also commissioned to paint the dome of St Paul's Cathedral (against Sir Christopher Wren's wishes) and the ceilings and staircases of many great country houses. Some of his best work in Oxford colleges has been superseded and destroyed. Thornhill (1675–1734) is perhaps more interesting for his connection with greater painters than on his own account. Thus he not only succeeded Kneller as a Piazza resident but also followed him to Great Queen Street as one of the directors of Kneller's academy of painting there. A group of these formed another academy in James Street which eventually succumbed to the rivalry of Hogarth's academy in St Martin's Lane. Hogarth himself was to marry Thornhill's daughter. Before his death Thornhill retired to Dorset, where he had been born. He was painted more than once by his great son-in-law, and this in itself is a form of immortality.

Another painter of high talent whose studio was in the Piazza was Richard Wilson (1714–1782) (Pl. 6), whose father was the incumbent of Penegoes in Montgomeryshire. He began as a portrait-painter but was advised, during a stay of six years in Italy, to turn to landscape instead. This he did, and the fame of his success preceded him to England, where he arrived in 1756. He painted a few famous pictures in England, yet his commissions, for some unexplained reason, were few. He never seems to have arrived at anything that could be called a heyday, his decline was long and slow, and his end was wretched. But he kept his pride and his belief in himself, and his reputation as a painter today justifies a prophecy that was made of him long, long ago by another Covent Garden resident, Dr Wolcot, who called himself Peter Pindar and was considered a great wit in his day:

> But, honest Wilson, never mind;
> Immortal praises thou shalt find,
> And for a dinner have no cause to fear.
> Thou start'st at my prophetic rhymes;
> Don't be impatient for those times;
> Wait till thou hast been dead a hundred year.

Wilson, in short, is now acknowledged to be one of the greatest English landscape-painters. His art was based upon that of Poussin and Claude. It was inspired by the scenery of the Italian Campagna with its pellucid skies and ancient ruins. And we may now read that 'in grandeur of design, in breadth of treatment, in the harmony of its rich but quiet colour, and in the rendering of space and air, Wilson has few rivals'— the few presumably including Crome and Turner.

Yet of all his contemporaries only the musician Dr Arne and the actor David Garrick seem to have liked Wilson's company. He was stout and robust, and in his later years his face was blotchy and his nose scarlet, apparently owing to his addiction to porter, or strong black beer. He is said to have declared porter to be his only luxury: 'His fondness for this beverage was so well-known that Zoffany introduced him with a pot of it at his elbow into his picture of the royal academicians (1773), but painted it out when Wilson threatened to thrash him. He was shy of society, especially when years of neglect and poverty had embittered him. He lived in and for his art, conscious in his own genius and scornful of the opinions of others. His spirit never broke; his faith never faltered; he made no concession to popular opinion, but fought for his own ideals to the last.'

Clearly a very Welsh Welshman!

Few even among his brother-painters befriended Wilson. He was supposed to be on bad terms even with the great Sir Joshua Reynolds, then king of portrait-painters and one who was as magnanimous as he could afford to be. This may have been because of an incident at a social gathering of academicians at the Turk's Head in Gerrard Street, not many yards out of this book's immediate circle. Just after Sir Joshua had proposed the health of Gainsborough as 'the best landscape-painter', Wilson audibly added 'and the best portrait-painter too', and Sir Joshua ignored the interruption. It is fair to add that, some years later when Wilson was in sore straits, Sir Joshua commissioned two pictures from him. It was another painter, the admirable and successful Paul Sandby, who recommended Wilson to important patrons when he was new to London and who purchased pictures from him when he became seriously ill-to-do. Besides being a bit of a Bardolph in his appearance, this rugged but sublime painter seems also to have had a little of Lear's Kent in his nature and bearing (or at least of the Kent as interpreted by the Duke of Cornwall):

> This is some fellow,
> Who, having been praised for bluntness, doth affect
> A saucy roughness, and constrains the garb
> Quite from his nature: he cannot flatter, he,—
> An honest mind and plain,—he must speak truth!
> ' An they will take it, so; if not, he's plain.

He also appears to have made the strategic mistake of asking too little for his pictures instead of too much. Anyhow he managed to live for several years in the Great Piazza, and then declined to meaner and meaner lodgings in the region of Charlotte Street, where the poorer sort of painters live in our own time. Eight years before his death Wilson painted a landscape of Cader Idris in North Wales which is quite simply one of the most dramatic of all British landscapes. The supreme art connoisseur of our own time, Sir Edward Marsh, in his old age and when he was undeniably ill-to-do himself, presented it in 1945 to the nation and it is now housed in the Tate Gallery. A more worldly minded man might have sold it for thousands of pounds. The Nation was perhaps too distracted at the time to seem particularly grateful.

A luckier and happier painter with Covent Garden connections was the aforementioned John Zoffany (1733–1810), some of whose best work survives in that thesaurus of theatrical paintings, the Garrick Club. Like Lely and Kneller a century earlier, he was a foreigner who made both his fortune and his reputation when he came to England. Not only was he a painter in whom all lovers of the old actors must take delight: born at Ratisbon in 1733, he could boast that his uncle was architect to the Prince of Thurn and Taxis (quite my favourite among all noble names). He toured Italy for twelve years and migrated to England in 1758. He did badly at first, and is said to have almost starved in a garret in Drury Lane. But fortunately another Italian immigrant came along to introduce him to a clock-maker called Rimbault of Great St Andrew Street in Seven Dials (just outside our appointed circle). Rimbault employed Zoffany to paint the faces of his Dutch clocks. Thereafter he became assistant to the theatrical portrait-painter Benjamin Wilson, and David Garrick himself is said to have detected the assistant's hand behind the master's. Wilson, incidentally, lived in Great Queen Street in the house and studio formerly occupied by Sir Godfrey Kneller. In course of time Zoffany became Garrick's favourite delineator in all his favourite roles. His portraits of the great actor as Abel Drugger in *The Alchemist*, Jaffier in *Venice Preserved*, Macbeth, and Sir John Brute in *The Provok'd Wife* are familiar enhancements of the Garrick Club.

Little is known of Zoffany's way of life. But it is certain that he joined the St Martin's Lane Academy in Peter's Court, and that he was an habitué of Old Slaughter's Coffee House. For a short time at least he had a studio in the Piazza auction-rooms (afterwards George Robins's). There he painted James Boswell and the comedian Samuel Foote in the part of Major Sturgeon in *The Mayor of Garratt*. In 1769 Zoffany became an academician, but he does not seem to have moved further up socially than Frith Street, Soho. He left England for Italy again in 1772. After seven years, during which time he became an Austrian Baron as a reward for his portrait of the Empress Maria Theresa, he returned to England only to leave it again in 1783 for seven years in India. A rolling stone that gathered moss!

He returned finally to England in 1790 with a swollen purse but diminished powers, and took a house in Strand-on-the-Green where he died in 1810. For St George's Church at Old Brentford he designed an altar-piece of The Last Supper in which he depicted himself as St Peter and various Strand-on-the-Green fishermen as the other Apostles. It is nice to know that this is still there. Zoffany was buried at Kew. He left fine portraits of Gainsborough, Charles Macklin the actor (another great Covent-Gardener), and George Steevens, the Shakespearean scholar.

Yet another resident, George Robins—in whose Piazza rooms

Zoffany had a studio—was for fifty years a celebrated auctioneer. The same premises were long occupied by his father, Henry Robins. No auctioneer has ever had greater praise than George Robins: 'The tact with which every advantage connected with the property he had to describe was seized upon and turned to profit in his glowing descriptions, and his ready wit and repartee in the rostrum, caused him to be one of the most successful and persuasive advocates in seducing his auditors to bid freely that ever appeared at the auction mart....' Perhaps no man in his station was ever more courted by his superiors; they profited by his advice and were amused by his eccentricities. In 1818 he exposed the bad management of the sub-committee of Drury Lane Theatre, and became the chief means of obtaining a new arrangement by which the house was released from debt. At a later period he helped to resuscitate the fortunes of Covent Garden Theatre. He was, too, a great advocate of the claims of comedians and their families to public sympathy. This George Robins was, in short, one of the earliest and best of the Friends of Covent Garden.

A very different sort of denizen of The Piazza—and only for a few years—was the actress-authoress-courtesan, Mrs Mary Robinson (1758–1800) (Pl. 7), who was nicknamed Perdita because that virginal innocent in Shakespeare's *Winter's Tale* was, curiously enough, her most successful feat of impersonation.

Not to mince matters—a habit, anyhow, which is direly out of fashion—'Perdita' was all that is meant by 'a flaunting extravagant quean', in Sir Harry Bumper's song in the Sheridan comedy. Born at Bristol in 1758 she came to a finishing school in London and when still a young girl was introduced to Garrick, who was much struck by her looks and said her voice reminded him of his favourite Mrs Cibber. Garrick's (Pl. 33) several biographers are cautious as to whether his interest in this young nymph was purely professional. One of the latest and best, Miss Margaret Barton, has surely a note of innuendo in her description of what happened:

'He had rehearsed her in the part of Cordelia, intending to act with her, but her sudden and unexpected marriage had wrecked his plans. While seeking re-engagement after the failure of her marriage, she had recited some of Juliet's speeches in the greenroom, and Garrick, who was present, urged Sheridan to present her in that role. At the rehearsals he coached her in every detail, often going through the whole of Romeo's part himself until he was completely exhausted; and on the night he sat in his old place in the orchestra to give her confidence. She pleased the audience well enough, but the beauty of her face, and, more particularly, her figure, which suited her for "breeches" parts, soon took her into comedy and thence to the Prince of Wales's protection.'

It is a fine, flaunting, extravagant, headlong sentence.

She had been secretly married at the age of sixteen to one Thomas Robinson, an articled clerk. The wedding was at St Martin's Church, and the couple lived for a time in Great Queen Street, at the north-east corner of the Covent Garden district. The site of the house where she lived first with her husband and then with her mother is now occupied by the Freemasons' Temple. For two years thereafter she lived in Hatton Garden, neglected by her husband and 'receiving compromising attentions from Lord Lyttelton and other rakes'. Subsequently she spent a period in gaol with her husband, who had been arrested for debt. She beguiled the time by writing ladylike verses, and when she came out of prison she recited them to Sheridan, who took her to see Garrick again. Garrick coached her, as we have seen, in Juliet, in which she made her mark at the age of eighteen. She left the stage at the age of twenty-two, playing among other parts in her last season, Viola, Rosalind and Perdita. All the famous painters of the day—including Reynolds and Gainsborough—vied with one another in painting the famous-infamous Perdita. Had she not been the Prince of Wales's mistress, and had not Charles James Fox, her succeeding protector, secured a pension for her? In her early heyday she was the general talk of Hyde Park. One day she would appear there in the guise of a peasant-girl, without make-up, in her own natural bloom. Next day she would appear in elegant toilette, 'trimmed, powdered, patched, painted to the utmost power of rouge and white lead'. A third day it was as an Amazon in cravat and jupon: 'But be she what she might, the hats of the fashionable promenaders swept the ground as she passed.' On a Sunday morning 'the style was a high phaeton, in which she was driven by the favoured of the day. Three candidates and her husband were outriders; and this in the face of the congregations turning out of places of worship'.

Perdita's establishment in Covent Garden before she moved further west was in the Little Piazza near the site of the Hummums Hotel. In her middle age she was afflicted with what appeared to be either palsy or arthritis or a mixture of the two, and she died in her forties, the date being 28th December 1800 and therefore—as I compute it—in the last week of the eighteenth century. Fifteen years later she still had champions. Hazlitt defended her against the personal animus of William Gifford, whom he called not only ungentlemanly but also unmanly; and Mrs Siddons in a letter written in 1793, still within Perdita's lifetime, has the sentiment: 'The charming and beautiful Mrs. Robinson! I pity her from the bottom of my soul.' But it is not clear whether Siddons was sympathizing with Perdita's malady or with the fact that her Prince Florizel had paid her off with a bond which was never honoured.

The eccentric but much more respectable Lady Mary Wortley Montagu (1689–1762) lived likewise in the Piazza for a time, since a letter from Pope is addressed to her there. Here, too, dwelt many other persons of high quality, many more painters and actors, and more than one notorious bawdy-house proprietor. It took all sorts to make the little world of Covent Garden.

The south side of the square, along which no piazza-wall was formed, is now represented by a newish street called Tavistock Street, first built around 1704. Here today is the splendid Lutyens-designed head-quarters of *Country Life*—of which more, a little later—and here a few doors to the east lived for more than thirty years that good writer, gracious woman, and notable playwright and novelist, Clemence Dane. (Mrs Patrick Campbell praised her in a letter to Bernard Shaw: 'Clemence Dane is a most dear woman and superlatively clever.') But a little to the north of this street, and facing it, was Tavistock Row, which is now merely a fenced-in shelter for wooden boxes, carts and lorries. It ran in a continuous line, westwards, from Henrietta Street. Here dwelt for a short time the socialist philosopher William Godwin, who was Shelley's father-in-law. Here lived and died the remarkable veteran actor Charles Macklin. He died in 1797 and swore he was born in the nineties of the previous century. In this row, too, dwelt a poor man called John Campbell, who paid nine shillings a week for two little rooms and finished up, long afterwards, as Lord Chancellor of England.

One of the row's first inhabitants was the Dutch marine painter, Willem Vandevelde, the younger, who had followed his father to England to paint sea-fights under royal patronage. He died at this address in 1707. Sixty years later there died in this same row Christian Friedrich Zincke, a distinguished enamellist and also a portrait-painter to the Walpole family. In the same house subsequently lived another painter, Nathaniel Dance, whose father, George Dance, was architect of the Mansion House and many other London buildings. His brother George rebuilt Newgate and was one of the original Royal Academicians. It would be pleasant to discover that these were ancestors of Sir George Dance, the librettist and manager, who contributed £30,000 to a fund to save the Old Vic. But I have, alas, been unable to establish any connection. In a garret of the selfsame house lived Dr Wolcot (Peter Pindar) from 1783 to 1805, a rhymester who wrote so much that he could hardly avoid an occasional felicity now and then—e.g. on Sleep:

> How sweet, though lifeless, yet with life to lie!
> And, without dying, O how sweet to die!

And again, on The Royal Academicians:

> What rage for fame attends both great and small!
> Better be damned than mentioned not at all!

Wolcot, an odd gadabout, was born in Devon, took a degree in medicine at Aberdeen and went to Jamaica, where he became physician-general. He returned to England to take holy orders, but instead practised medicine at Truro in Cornwall, where he discovered a young painter of genius and brought him to London. This was John Opie. After launching and quarrelling with Opie, he took to versifying, on which he subsisted for nearly thirty years. In old age he became blind and had his head shaved; and Hazlitt in an out-of-the-way essay said of him that 'he looked like a venerable father of poetry or an unworthy son of the church'. He kept and treasured some sketches by Richard Wilson even though he could not see them, saying he preferred them to Claude—unlike Hazlitt, who thought Wilson lost by comparison.

Tavistock Street, as distinct from the vanished Tavistock Row, has far fewer memories and associations. But it was once considerably wider and full of fashionable shops. Clemence Dane, herself its best-remembered resident, has described it 'at its best never more than a modish shopping-centre'. Today, and indeed for the last sixty years, its chief claim to eminence is the superb building which houses the offices of *Country Life,* that most noble and consistent of weekly journals which performs, in the words of the architect himself, 'a useful service to that wide community devoted to the beauties and traditions of England'. The journal was founded in the year 1897—the year of Queen Victoria's Diamond Jubilee. In 1905 the present building was commissioned from Lutyens by the journal's founder, the late Edward Hudson. It was the great architect's very first work in London, his first public building and his first display of what he called his 'Wrenaissance' style. In the issue celebrating the seventieth anniversary of the journal a leading article pointed out how the paper has consistently supported a progressive policy in agriculture and repeatedly given aid to the preservation of the countryside and to nature conservation: 'But its greatest impact has probably been in the sphere of architecture and design: not merely by recording great houses while they were still lived in by their owners and while their contents were still intact; but by promoting good standards of design in the building of smaller houses and cottages and by sympathetic yet forthright assessment of new trends.' Edward Hudson, *the* Hudson, founder and editor of this distinguished paper with the distinguished office, had formerly owned the Southwark printing firm of Hudson and Kearns. In his commendable book, *The Strand Magazine 1891–1950,* Reginald Pound gives a vivid picture of his grandeur and individuality: 'Hudson is recalled by some for his huge high-roofed Rolls-Royce, with its folding steps on the running-board and twin red-throated exhaust funnels on the bonnet; by others for his daily habit of striding fearlessly across The Strand, hand imperiously upraised as a traffic signal, as he went to lunch at the Cecil or the Savoy.'

We may leave the Piazza by way of what little is left of the Tavistock Hotel on the northern side of the square. Sadly little, for only a block of new offices remains of the famous building demolished in the twenties just before I came to London. Near here was the Bedford Coffee-House, and many other such, frequented in their day by Steele and Addison, by Pope and Dryden, and later by Garrick and Sheridan. The Piazza Coffee-House later became the Piazza Hotel; Charles Dickens stayed there in 1844 and again in 1846. Its site is now occupied by the Floral Hall. The Tavistock Hotel's best remembrancer was my veteran editor, James Bone. Not only would he have liked me to quote him on the subject; he would have been huffed if I did not:

'Like several of London's architectural treasures, the Piazza at Covent Garden was little known to Londoners and difficult for strangers to find. Although it was the only remaining fragment of the great arcaded square which Inigo Jones designed, it had somehow avoided the attention of the guide-book writer.' This bears out what I have already said about the guides and the guide-books failing to realize that the sham portico of St Paul's Church with its coffee-stall (day and night) is the first-act setting of Shaw's *Pygmalion* and the place where Eliza first met Professor Henry Higgins; and, too, the scene of a painting by Hogarth. Here also Samuel Pepys watched a Punch and Judy show on 9th May 1662 and returned with his wife two weeks later.

J. B. continues:

'Even when the fragment was swept away to make space for the widening of Covent Garden Market its end received little publicity. It was only the eastern portion of the north piazza that was original, the western part, which runs from James Street to the seventeenth-century house [later the National Sporting Club, which is practically in King Street] being a nineteenth-century rebuilding. The part occupied by the Tavistock Hotel had the original Inigo Jones arcade of brick with plaster cover, but the upper part had been partly rebuilt. The dining-room of the hotel, which occupied the whole of the first floor over the arcade, was a long, low room in three parts that suggested the great architect in the grace and dignity of its proportions, although there were no mantelpieces or panelling left, and the aspect of the house generally was Early Victorian. In the ground floor the look of a coaching hotel persisted, and the street buffet had on its worn old brass apron the words "Cigar Divan"— the last in London to bear that inscription.'

Such vestiges are precious and would, in a wholly enlightened community, be preserved. By a happy fluke there is still—at the moment of writing—to be seen a legend at least a century old, high up on the wall of the south-west corner of the main market-building (Pl. 5). It reads:

JAS. BUTLER, HERBALIST & SEEDSMAN, LAVENDER WATER &C.

And it is a relic of the days when one went to Covent Garden to buy not only flowers and fruits and vegetables, but also spices, herbs and flavourings.

One had always understood that the Tavistock Hotel was one 'for gentlemen only', but James Bone put us right on this subject:

'For more than a century the hotel had been the London rendezvous for naval officers, and Japhet, in Captain Marryat's diverting book, stayed there. [So, too, incidentally, did Captain Marryat himself on occasion. And so did Edward FitzGerald who made the reputation of Omar Khayyam.] It had always been known as a bachelor hotel, but before the First War the rule was relaxed through circumstances connected with the earlier Australian cricket teams. These teams put up at the Tavistock, and when they brought their wives with them they persuaded the management to relax its rule. But it was to the end almost entirely a masculine hotel. It held to its old ways, and even the First War did not make it quite like other hotels, although it did away with the large Early Victorian bowls in which coffee and tea were served in the morning to a burly and energetic crowd of patrons from the Market outside who were usually taking their lunch when other people were coming down to breakfast.'

This tendency persists in the half-dozen taverns within the market that are open from seven till nine every morning 'for market-workers only'. In most of them food is served—hot bacon sandwiches for preference—and tea and coffee also, though oftener than not it is laced with whisky or rum.

Bone speculates on what became of the permanent residents of the Tavistock Hotel, 'that picturesque and historical caravanserai'. It had many bedrooms, some of them exceptionally large and lofty, in which strange old gentlemen resided, sometimes for years on end: 'Some of them, it was said, never came out of their bedrooms at all except at night, sometimes visiting the National Sporting Club [a minute's walk away at the beginning of King Street] but usually perambulating round the Garden, poking the fruit and vegetables as farmers do pigs.' He recalls one of these, an old Crown Colony gentleman who accumulated in his bedroom a huge pyramid of used collars which nobody was allowed to touch. He perpetuates Alfred, 'the famous slim and lordly head-waiter, who had been there for forty years and remembered the early Australian cricketers and fine, whiskered men they were,' including Bannerman, Spofforth, and all the other heroes. 'He could remember much more than he would care to say. Alfred was quite unperturbed about the end of the hotel. One wondered if in the end he went to some fine appropriate place where that old anemometer instrument (connected with the vane on the top of the Tavistock to tell how the wind was blowing) kept him company. One knew of no other hotel with such an instrument. It dated back to the days when the East Indiamen sailed from Gravesend, and men of the period sat in the coffee-room watching the instrument for a favourable wind, and possibly dreading it, while they enjoyed their Tom-and-Jerry life in London. . . .' It was in this same room that the Rabelais Club, with Walter Besant, novelist and historian of all that was decorous, as chairman, held its first dinner. The Club was intended as 'a declaration of virility' in literature, and Thomas Hardy was one of the diners.

Lastly, Bone tells us how he went to the sale of the hotel's furnishings, and noted how the eighteenth-century portrait of a gentleman in blue and buff 'stolidly regarded the hordes of small dealers'. It was catalogued simply as 'Portrait of a Gentleman—English School'. But it was known to be a portrait of the original Mr Harrison who founded the Tavistock Hotel in the late eighteenth century, and whose family held it till 1886. His name stood till the end in raised letters over the entrance.

As a tail-piece to this chapter let me transcribe two highly relevant pages from John Thomas Smith's *Nollekens and his Times* which first appeared in 1828, just a century before the closure of the Tavistock Hotel. It is an account of a morning walk in the Market, taken by Nollekens and Mrs Nollekens, Mrs Carter and Smith himself, and the encounters they had. The conversations that resulted from these encounters take us right back into the eighteenth century and give some amusing sidelights on certain quaint customs and observances.

A few notes are necessary for the ordinary reader's perfect appreciation of this passage. Nollekens himself, of Flemish origin, was a mean and cheese-paring little dwarf and yet a sculptor of high talent and in high places. He excelled in modelling life-size busts, and he has left likenesses of most of his famous contemporaries—Garrick, Fox, Pitt, Laurence Sterne, Goldsmith, Dr Johnson, King George III. He also left a fortune of over £200,000, but most of it in tiny moieties to people like his apprentice and model, John Thomas Smith himself, who had every honest reason to expect a large bequest. His wife was tall, thin and straight (in strong contrast to her husband), but also incredibly mean and eccentric, which may explain why the marriage appears to have been a grotesquely happy one. Both looked as though drawn and painted by Rowlandson.

Mrs Elizabeth Carter, a friend of both, was the celebrated blue-stocking, esteemed by both Dr Johnson and his Boswell, a formidable linguist and the translator of Epictetus. She lived on till 1806, dying in her eighty-ninth year. She was 'a noble-looking woman', according to Fanny Burney, but also human and likeable, according to Johnson: 'Mrs. Carter can make a pudding as well as translate Epictetus.' Here then is the highly informative evocative passage from John Thomas Smith's account of himself and of his extraordinary com-panions. His book is highly unequal. If it were all as vivid as this unaltered and unshortened extract, it would be more easily accessible.

'One spring morning as I was passing through Covent-garden, I was accosted by Mrs. Elizabeth Carter, who had accompanied Mrs. Nollekens thither for the purpose of purchasing some roots of dandelion, an infusion of which had been strongly recommended to her husband by Dr. Jebb. Twigg, the Fruiterer, to whom Mr. Justice Welch, during his magistracy, had often been kind, was at all times gratefully attentive to Miss Welch and her sister, Mrs. Nollekens. He procured the roots she wanted from that class of people called "Simplers" who sit in the centre of the garden. The fruiterer was a talkative man and was called by some of his jocular friends the "Twig of the Garden"; he had been cook at the Shakespeare Tavern, and knew all the wits and eccentric characters of his early days.

'Mrs. Carter, though she was seldom fond of noticing strangers, fell by degrees into a conversation with Twigg, and asked him which house it was in Tavistock-row that Miss Wray, who was shot by the Rev. James Hackman, occupied before she resided with Lord Sandwich; to which he replied, "It was that on the south-west corner of Tavistock-court, next to the one in which the famous Willem Vandevelde, the Marine-painter, died." This corner house, No. 4, is now occupied by a tailor; and that in which Vandevelde lived, now No. 5, is inhabited by Irish Johnstone, as he is usually called, that once delightful actor and excellent portrayer of the characters of Irishmen. "Pray," continued the lady, "which was

Zincke's, the celebrated Enameller's?" "Why, Ma'am," said he, "it is No. 13, that in which Mr. Nathaniel Dance, the Painter, afterwards lived. Meyer, another famous Miniature-painter, resided in it; and the garrets are now occupied by Peter Pindar." [Doctor Wolcot.] "I recollect, Ma'am," continued the fruiterer, "Old Joe, who was the first person who sold flowers in this Garden: his stand was at that corner within the enclosure, then called Primrose Hill, opposite to Lowe's Hotel." (This spot was so named in consequence of its being the station of those persons who brought primroses to the Garden.) "Lowe had been a hair-dresser in Tavistock-street before he took that large house, which he established as a family hotel, the earliest of that description in London, where he distributed medals,[1] which procured him many lodgers." Mrs. Nollekens then requested to know which house it was in James-street, where her father's old friend, Mr. Charles Grignon, resided; the engraver so extensively, and for so many years, employed upon the designs of Gravelot, Hayman, and Wale. "No. 27," said Twigg; "I recollect the old house when it was a shop inhabited by two old Frenchwomen, who came over here to chew paper for the *papier-mâché* people." Mrs. Nollekens: "Ridiculous! I think Mr. Nollekens once told me that the elder Wilton, Lady Chambers's grandfather, was the person who employed people from France to work in the *papier-mâché* manufactory, which he established in Edward-street, Cavendish-square." Twigg: "I can assure you, Ma'am, these women bought the paper-cuttings from the stationers and book-binders, and produced it in that way, in order to keep it a secret, before they used our machine for mashing it." Mrs. Carter: "I recollect, Sir, when Mr. Garrick acted, hackney-chairs were then so numerous, that they stood all round the Piazzas, down Southampton-street, and extended more than half-way along Maiden-lane, so much were they in requisition at that time." Twigg: "Then, I suppose, Ma'am, you also recollect the shoe-blacks at every corner of the streets, whose cry was 'Black your shoes, your Honour'?" "Yes, Sir, perfectly well; and the clergyman of your parish walking about and visiting the fruit-shops in the Garden in his canonicals; and I likewise remember a very portly woman sitting at her fruit-stall in a dress of lace, which it was said cost at least one hundred guineas, though a greater sum was often mentioned."

[1] Lowe's 'medals' were metal discs engraved for advertising purposes.

'Here this dialogue about old times ended, by the entrance of several other customers; upon which Mrs. Carter and Mrs. Nollekens left the shop to pay a morning visit to Mrs. Garrick, and I made my bow.'

This last was David Garrick's widow who was to live on to the great age of ninety-eight. At that age she had travelled to London from Hampton Court in order to see some alterations that had been made at Drury Lane Theatre. While she was resting in her chair before setting out for the theatre her maid handed her a cup of tea. 'Put it down, hussy,' she said irritably; 'do you think I cannot help myself?' They were her last words. The maid put down the tea and left her mistress to help herself. When she came back a few minutes later, Mrs Garrick was dead.

CHAPTER THREE

ARIAS AND FLOWERS

The top or quarter-segment of our circle is bounded on the north by the full length of Long Acre stretching for something like a quarter-mile from its western end which might be called 'St Martin's Circle', for at this point Garrick Street, St Martin's Lane, Cranbourn Street, Great Newport Street, Upper St Martin's Lane and Long Acre itself all converge. At its other eastern extreme Long Acre crosses Drury Lane to become Great Queen Street—the latter such a history-laden thoroughfare that we shall be tempted to take in a yard or two of it when we arrive there.

The other boundaries of our segment are Garrick Street as far as Floral Street and along the latter for its whole length to Bow Street, and along Broad Court as far as Drury Lane, which is our eastern boundary. The streets taken in by this outline are the north end of the comparatively modern Garrick Street; narrow and ancient Floral Street (formerly Hart Street), which runs parallel to Long Acre; the short James Street, which runs south from Long Acre to the Piazza; the fairly new Mart Street at the back of the Opera House; Bow Street, running north and south, into which the Opera House faces; and Broad Court, which is again parallel to 'The Acre', as the porters call Long Acre. Facing the façade of the Opera (a major European opera house) is perhaps the best-known police station in the world, that of Bow Street. Within this segment are a few decent private apartments, a few vestigial slum residences, a vast amount of market offices and warehouses, the headquarters of several famous publishing houses, half-a-dozen old and time-honoured taverns.

Long Acre has always been a little dull and eventless in comparison with the congeries of lesser streets and courts and alleys behind it. It began as an avenue of elm trees, and when it became a populated street its business concern was largely with coach-builders and eventually with motor cars. Pepys in his Diary tells us how he went to Long Acre on one occasion to buy a coach, 'a coach just like Povy's, but it was sold this very morning'. He also occasionally visited his father-in-law, who lived in this street. At night he was sometimes inclined to haunt the neighbourhood for less respectable purposes. The pleasantest possible verification of the fact that the best and most opulent coaches were built in Long Acre is to be found in Anthony Trollope's *Dr Thorne*, in the passage where Augusta Gresham's condition is described after she had been jilted by the very rich but not otherwise very desirable Mr Moffat: 'She neither raved nor fainted, nor walked about by moonlight alone. She wrote no poetry, and never once thought of suicide. When, indeed, she remembered the rosy-tinted lining, the unfathomable softness of that Long-acre carriage, her spirit did for one moment give way, but, on the whole, she bore it as a strong-minded woman and a De Courcy should do.'

In older times Long Acre's eminent inhabitants were very few, but those few were eminent indeed. Oliver Cromwell lived on its south side for six years, from 1637 to 1643; so, at least, the topographical chronicles say, though history tells us that it was in exactly those years that Cromwell was organizing his Ironsides and fighting in the Civil War—at Edgehill (1642) and at Marston Moor (1644). Can 'Captain Cromwell' who 'was rated to the poor of St Martin's at 10s 10d' be someone other than Oliver? Whatever this soldier's identity his neighbour was the sculptor Nicholas Stone, who specialized in tombs and designed, among many others, that of Dr John Donne in his winding sheet in St Paul's Cathedral.

He had three sons—Henry, a painter, and Nicholas and John, both sculptors. All were buried in their family vault in St Martin-in-the-Fields. Henry's portrait was painted by Sir Peter Lely; a portrait of Nicholas the younger was in the possession of Colley Cibber. John, who became a Cavalier, narrowly escaped hanging, hid for some months in the Long Acre house without his father's knowledge, eventually escaped to France, and returned in 1667 just after the Restoration to die in his father's dwelling as the last of the family. John Dryden, poet, playwright and satirist, lived for four years (1682-6) in a house opposite Rose Street.

One of the more interesting landmarks in Long Acre was on its north side near its eastern extremity, on what was until lately the site of

Odhams Press and the *Sun* newspaper. This was a building called St Martin's Hall, designed by Richard Westmacott, and built by John Hullah, whose name I noticed in my infancy as the composer of such strongly emotional Victorian ballads as *The Sands of Dee* and *Three Fishers Went Sailing* (to words of Charles Kingsley). John Hullah, born at Worcester in 1812, came to be known as 'the pioneer of music for the people'. He collaborated with his friend Charles Dickens in a quite successful opera, *The Village Coquettes*, the score of which was later destroyed in a fire. Hullah organized highly popular singing classes in Exeter Hall, and moved them to this new hall in Long Acre in 1850. It was so used for some ten years. But the hall is even more notable for the fact that it was here that Dickens gave his very first series of readings. Over the four previous years he had given odd readings of his own works for charity. For his own benefit he now planned a series of sixteen recitals at the St Martin's Hall spread over the period from 29th April to 22nd July 1858.

Their success was the talk of London. Early in the course he wrote to the great Macready, who was now in retirement: 'The St Martin's Hall audience was a very extraordinary thing. The two thousand odd people were like one, and their enthusiasm was something awful.' Good to see the last word used in its old true sense of awe-inspiring! A second series of these readings was planned for the year 1861. They duly took place at the St James's Hall in Piccadilly (where the Piccadilly Hotel now stands). For meanwhile the St Martin's Hall in Long Acre had been burned to the ground. It was subsequently rebuilt as a playhouse called the Queen's Theatre. Later, about the year 1879, this theatre became the headquarters of the Clerical Co-operative Stores, and later still it was used as a gymnasium by the Young Men's Christian Association. But till the end, before it became Odhams Press, the building had the look of a theatre, and I can remember in the very late twenties detecting parts of the legend 'Queen's Theatre' on the fanlight of what used to be the façade, even though it had ceased to be such as long ago as 1887. It had opened as a theatre in 1867, when its proprietor was Henry Labouchere and its manager Alfred Wigan. It had a short but lively career. The first play was an adaptation of Charles Reade's novel *White Lies*. There appears to have been a regular company at the Queen's, and among the distinguished players who appeared with it were Henry Irving, J. L. Toole, Charles Wyndham, John Clayton, Henrietta Hodson, Lionel Brough and

Ellen Terry. Tommaso Salvini played his great Othello there in 1875, and John Coleman played Shakespeare's Henry V there in 1876. It was a notably large theatre, with only Covent Garden and Drury Lane superior in size. At its opening it was lavishly decorated by the painter Albert Moore, mainly known, in Miss Marguerite Steen's phrase, 'for his grouping of young women in pseudo-Greek costumes, cuddling sprays of apple blossom on chilly marble benches'.

It was in this company that Henry Irving first met Ellen Terry, destined to become his leading lady at the Lyceum from 1878 till the very end of the century. At the Queen's they played together only in one production, that of Garrick's reduced version of *The Taming of the Shrew*. This was in support of two farces played by J. L. Toole, the comedian, who was Irving's great friend. Irving's Petruchio was severely criticized, and the little play had no great success. He had as yet to acquire anything like the technique of his partner, who left the stage for nearly six years just after this engagement. She went to the country, into Hertfordshire, and bore her two children, Edith and Gordon Craig, to the architect Edward William Godwin.

It is odd to note that Irving and Ellen Terry saw little to admire in each other at their first meeting. The actress wrote in her auto-biography:

'One very foggy night in December, 1867, I acted for the first time with Henry Irving. This was a great event in my life, but at the time it passed me by and left "no wrack behind".... Until I went to the Lyceum Theatre, Henry Irving was nothing to me and I was nothing to him. I never consciously thought that he would become a great actor. He had no high opinion of *my* acting! He has said since that he thought me at the Queen's Theatre charming and individual as a woman, but as an actress *hoydenish*! I believe that he had hardly spared me even so much definite thought as this. His soul was not more surely in his body than in the theatre, and I, a woman who was at this time caring more about love and life than the theatre, must have been to him more or less unsympathetic. ... He had it all in him when we acted together that foggy night, but he could express very little. Many of his defects sprang from his not having been on the stage as a child. He was stiff with self-conscious-ness; his eyes were dull, his face heavy. The piece we played was Garrick's boiled-down version of *The Taming of the Shrew*, and he, as

Petruchio, appreciated the humour and everything else far more than I did; and how much more to blame *I* was, for I was at this time much more easy and skilful from a technical point of view. . . . Henry Irving, when he played Petruchio, had been toiling in the provinces for eleven years, and not until Rawdon Scudamore in *Hunted Down* had he had any success. Even that was forgotten in his failure as Petruchio. What a trouncing he received from the critics who have since heaped praise on many worse players!'

At the end of the same season a preposterous melodrama called *The Lancashire Lass* was put on. A fine old character-actor, Sam Emery, saved the play from the condemnation it deserved. But a distinguished spectator in the audience discerned another and a potentially fine actor in the company. He said to his family round the supper table when he got home from the Queen's Theatre: 'But there was a young fellow in the play who sits at the table with Sam Emery and is bullied by him; the young fellow's name is Henry Irving and if he some day doesn't come out as a great actor I know nothing of the art.' This was none other than Charles Dickens, who was clearly more perceptive than Ellen Terry herself.

Opening into Long Acre on the south side, as we proceed from west to east, are the following alleys and thoroughfares: Rose Street, Conduit Court, Banbury Court, Langley Court, James Street, Hanover Place, Bow Street, Broad Court, and finally Drury Lane itself. The streets are, of course, the more important, but each little alley has its associations. Each leads into Floral Street; James Street crosses it to proceed into the north end of the Piazza; Bow Street crosses it to descend into The Strand (by which time it has become Wellington Street, formerly called Brydges Street). Rose Street, after crossing Floral Street, has a crooked continuation into Garrick Street by way of an ancient and picturesque tavern called The Lamb and Flag. To this we may return for its own sake as well as for the fact that its present enlightened landlord collects Drydeniana.

In Rose Street John Dryden was beaten up by three hired bullies on a night in 1679 when he was on his way home from Will's Coffee House (Pl. 13) to his home in Long Acre. The victim offered, and deposited in Child's Bank in Fleet Street, a reward of £50 for information as to his assailants. It is probable but not proved that the assault was planned and ordered by the Earl of Rochester in revenge for a passage in Lord Mulgrave's *Essay on Satire*, a passage which Rochester wrongly attributed to Dryden.

Another inhabitant of Rose Street for a time was that singular and somewhat sinister bookseller called Edmund Curll, whom Pope immortalized in *The Dunciad*—if truly it be immortality to be castigated in the least readable of Pope's major works. Their quarrel is both mysterious and tedious, since Pope's share in the scrap is almost as questionable as Curll's, though, of course, Pope, being a writer by trade, had the last word. Curll was a bookseller and publisher with a partiality for obscenities. The word 'curlicism' in his time became a synonym for literary indecency. He was a queer fish who began his London career with a system of newspaper quarrels in order to bring himself into public notice. He would do almost anything to get talked about. 'Dauntless Curll', Pope called him, and there is a sarcastic footnote in *The Dunciad* which begins: 'We come now to a character of much respect, Mr Edmund Curl [*so spelt*]. As a plain repetition of great actions is the best praise of them, we shall only say of this eminent man that he carried the Trade many lengths beyond what it ever before had arrived at, and that he was the envy and admiration of all his profession. He possesst himself of a command over all authors whatever; he caus'd them to write what he pleas'd; they could not call their very names their own . . .'

Curll, it seems, was incurable. He was reprimanded by the House of Lords, imprisoned for five months, placed in the pillory, tossed in a blanket by the Westminster Boys, and pestered with scorn by Pope and others. But dauntlessly he continued into hideous old age. He is variously described in contemporary chronicles as tall, thin and ugly, as splayfooted and 'baker-kneed', with eyes that were large, projecting, goggling and purblind. He was not an infidel, but certainly a debauchee, and it is something of a highlight to the picture to be told that no man could talk better on theatrical subjects. He published a large number of books of his own, but it was his occasional habit to produce a volume—his *Court Poems*, for example—some of which he lyingly attributed to famous poets like Pope in order to get the volume sold. From the start of his long career he fully realized the commercial value of scandal and impudence. He had the 'cheek' to call his bookshop in Rose Street The Pope's Head. He died there in 1747 and was buried in St Paul's, Covent Garden. Writing to Swift about his twenty years' quarrel with Curll, Pope complained of the unworthiness of this particular enemy, and has a phrase—I have wasted many pleasurable hours trying to trace it but know that it exists—to the effect that he would much rather be hit by a thunderbolt than by a piss-pot such as Curll.

In Rose Street, too, lived and died Samuel Butler the first, the one who wrote a mock-epic called *Hudibras* which even men-of-letters do not, as a rule, admit to have read *in toto*. The general reader—and many a man-of-letters also—is quite content to read *this* Samuel Butler serendipitously—i.e. to read amusedly through the page or two devoted to him in the quotation-books while searching for something else. Thus, and only thus, most of us are familiar with pithy couplets like:

> He that complies against his will,
> Is of his own opinion still.

And this, which combines the neatness of Pope with the ingenuity of Browning:

> The best of all our actions tend
> To the preposterousest end.

Thus, too, we can claim to have read at least the first two lines of *Hudibras* which run:

> When civil fury first grew high,
> And men fell out they knew not why—

though we may not be beguiled to take up the mock-epic itself to discover exactly of whom it is written that they

> Compound for sins they are inclined to
> By damning those they have no mind to!

This witty Butler, whose life extended between 1612 and 1680, was the son of a Worcestershire farmer who went to either Oxford or Cambridge or possibly both; became a clerk and factotum to various persons of quality; spent his leisure in music and painting; and after the Restoration became steward at Ludlow Castle. *Hudibras* appeared in three parts between 1663 and 1678 and was much relished by King Charles II, who sent the poet £300 when he heard he was indigent. Butler died 'of a consumption' and was buried in the churchyard of St Paul's, Covent Garden. Hazlitt had no end of admiration, and quotes more Butler than can be found in the quotation-books—this, for example, on the self-declared master of many tongues:

> Yet he that is but able to express
> No sense at all in several languages,
> Will pass for learneder than he that's known
> To speak the strongest reason in his own.

Hazlitt has elsewhere an admirable summary of Butler which, all the same, tends surely to overpraise his wit: 'Butler (the author of *Hudibras*) has undoubtedly more wit than any other writer in the language. He has little besides to recommend him, if we except strong sense, and a laudable contempt of absurdity and hypocrisy. He has little story, little character, and no great humour in his singular poem. The invention of the fable seems borrowed from *Don Quixote*. He has however prodigious merit in his style, and in the fabrication of his rhymes.'

In this part of Long Acre—at No. 12—now stands the busy and friendly shop of Edward Stanford, the only business of my acquaintance which concentrates on maps and guide-books and what may be called the literature of travel. The next opening into the same street, going eastward, is Conduit Court. This used to flank the ancient and picturesque Bird in Hand Tavern which was inexcusably pulled down around 1954 and replaced with nothing of the slightest interest. I lived next door but one to this tavern—at No. 20 Long Acre—for nearly five years, and its landlord, a shrewd old Welshman named Arthur Powell, was my good friend. He had bushy grey eyebrows and a notable resemblance to the late Lord Beaverbrook. After his pub was destroyed he emigrated to British Columbia and died there in 1953. He will reappear in this book in very singular circumstances, directly connected with a ghost, a very distinguished ghost indeed, which I saw and which Arthur Powell helped me to identify. But that true story must await its proper place, which is a particular part of The Strand in the middle of the Second World War (see chapter five).

The side-entrance of The Bird in Hand was on the right as one went down Conduit Court. On the left were two old-fashioned shops with bay windows as I remember. In the first was an old cobbler who did small repairs for me, and he told me one day, quite casually, that the great Sir Henry Irving himself used to come in occasionally, on his walk from the West End to the Lyceum, to have a minor repair to his heel or his sole. In the second shop was a nice old chap who sold papers and old books, and finished up as a messenger for the *Illustrated London News* of which I was film-critic for twenty-one years (1947–68). Both of these old shops were demolished shortly after The Bird in Hand, leaving nothing of note or interest to replace them.

Banbury Court, next along, is featureless today, containing nothing but the backsides of warehouses. But in its immediate vicinity once upon a time was the Duke's Bagnio, the most considerable of the district's many private bath-houses which so easily degenerated into brothels. This one was built in 1682, and was later called the Queen's Bagnio and other names besides. Hereabouts at one time was another narrow passage off Long Acre with the alluring name of Leg Alley. But this may have been an earlier appellation for Banbury Court.

Farther east is James Street with the Covent Garden Underground Station at its north-western corner. James Street, though short, is longer than the other lanes and alleys I have mentioned since it does not terminate in Floral Street, but crosses it to proceed right into the Piazza in the middle of its northern side.

Charles Grignion, a famous line-engraver, lived for many years in James Street and was indeed born in Russell Street a few yards away (1717). He devoted himself to book illustration. Hogarth thought highly of him and employed him as engraver. In his ninetieth year a subscription was raised for his support, and he died at ninety-four. The destitution to which he was reduced was one of the causes that led to the foundation of the Artists' Benevolent Fund. In James Street also, 'at a house on the west side', lived Sir Henry Herbert (1595–1673), a Master of the Revels, and brother of 'blessed' George Herbert, the supreme metaphysical poet, and also of Lord Herbert of Cherbury. This Herbert was staying in his brother's great house at Wilton when King James visited it and knighted him and created him Master of the Revels. He took his duties seriously, claiming the right to license every kind of public entertainment throughout England. The earliest entries in his register concern exhibitions of beavers, elephants, dromedaries and performances by quack doctors. He also licensed public games, books and dramatic performances. He was, in essence and fact, the first Public Censor. The new king, Charles I, gave him sympathetic assistance in his reading of plays. After the Civil War and the Restoration he resumed his office as Censor and as Master of the Revels. Sir Henry was more difficult and demanding than any of the many who succeeded him in his contentious office. When in 1660 King Charles II granted licences to Thomas Killigrew and Sir William Davenant (Pl. 8) to erect two new playhouses with new companies (Drury Lane and Covent Garden) Sir Henry petitioned against the grant; and brought suits against them to recover fees due to his office. He also endeavoured to close the Cockpit Theatre in Drury Lane, which John Rhodes had opened without a licence from him. In 1661 King Charles II issued an order generally confirming Sir Henry's privileges. One way and another this original Censor lived 'a life of sturt and strife', like Robert Burns's Macpherson. He died in 1673 and was buried in St Paul's, Covent Garden. In James Street his was 'the last house but one from the corner of Hart Street' (now Floral Street). So it must have been alongside the White Lion Tavern, whose amiable landlord, the late Jack Hutton, was a goodly friend of mine.

Hogarth's father-in-law, Sir James Thornhill, who lived in the Piazza, also had a school of painting which was in James Street, on the east side. Next door to it were Langford's Auction Rooms (previously Robins's, and subsequently Cox's). Later, on the same ground was built the Tavistock Hotel, already described in the preceding chapter.

Floral Street (formerly Hart Street) runs, as we have indicated, from Garrick Street to Bow Street, and parallel to Long Acre. Here dwelt a notable actor and general man of the theatre of his day, Joseph Haines. Born in Covent Garden, he was educated at the school of St Martin-in-the-Fields, and was sent at the expense of some gentleman who admired his juvenile brightness to the Queen's College, Oxford. This served to make the brightness greater still, for he was soon chosen as Latin secretary to Sir Joseph Williamson, a Fellow of the college. But the brightness was diminished when he was dismissed for an unspecified fault of discretion, and young Haines joined a troupe of comedians at Stourbridge. He soon found his way to London and as a dancer caught the eye and the commendation of Pepys; also of Dryden, who chose him to play the comic servant in *The Assignation*. In 1673 he was the original Sparkish in Wycherley's *The Country Wife*, one of the wittiest and raciest plays of the Restoration, which has one scene set in the Piazza itself. Haines's exceptional education qualified him to write many prologues and epilogues, though he never seems to have tackled playwriting. He became a favourite actor of George

Farquhar and appeared in the first performances of the latter's *Love and a Bottle* and *The Inconstant*. Joe Haines died in his lodgings in Hart Street and was buried in St Paul's, Covent Garden. Cibber, in his solitary reference to him, calls him a 'wicked wit'.

In Floral Street, also, Charles Macklin at one time kept an extraordinary 'ordinary' in which he was his own master of ceremonies. But the enterprise failed and left the old actor, then in retirement, bankrupt. Macklin is a character who is bound to recur repeatedly in any survey of the Covent Garden district. He acted in and around it for at least sixty of his hundred years. He has been called 'the contemporary of the eighteenth century'. He lived and flourished side by side with Cibber and Barton Booth, he was the companion, rival and occasional enemy of Quin and Garrick, and he was still upon the stage, the stage of life at least, when the Kembles played in London.

That part of Floral Street which connects James Street with Bow Street could hardly be more quintessentially theatrical. On the left we begin with the Nag's Head Tavern (Pl. 35) which its owners, Messrs Whitbread, have since the late 'forties transmogrified into something that is—according to one's reason for entering—a pub, a restaurant, and a theatrical museum. Its sole adornments are theatrical and operatic playbills, prints and programmes. Its customers are of infinite variety since it is the 'local' of the Opera House itself—porters, market-salesmen, actors, musicians, dancers, singers, socialites, riff-raff rich and poor, layabouts and play-abouts, balletomanes, ballet-masters, composers, critics, more market-salesmen and more porters. The Nag's Head deserves a chapter to itself but it cannot have one, the more's the pity. On the same side of the street are store-rooms belonging to the Opera House and also Hanover Place, the last of the alleys debouching into Long Acre before we reach Drury Lane. Hanover Place is featureless now, but it was built as long ago as 1637; originally called Phoenix Alley, it had a tavern called The Crown (later The Ship), kept by John Taylor who was known as the Water Poet. He was an eccentric ex-sailor and odd-fish who is even less read nowadays than Samuel (Hudibras) Butler, one who does not particularly reward the general reader even casually, in the quotation books, though he is there credited with one incontrovertible line: ''Tis a mad world, my masters.' It is true that the *Dictionary of National Biography* devotes thirteen columns to John Taylor, but more than nine of these are taken up with the mere titles of his innumerable pamphlets and travelogues, and his

essential quality is summed up in a paragraph of barely fifty words:
'Although Taylor complacently styled himself the "king's water-poet"
and the "queen's water-man", he can at best be regarded only as a
literary bargee. As literature his books—many of them coarse and
brutal—are contemptible; but his pieces accurately mirror his age,
and are of great value to the historian and antiquary.'

Born at Gloucester in the year 1580, he was as a boy pressed into
the Navy and served at Flores in the Azores—but not with Grenville.
He was latterly, in fact, a tavern-keeper to trade, first in Oxford and
then at The Crown in Phoenix Alley. He died here, childless and
intestate, in 1653 and was buried in the churchyard of St Martin-in-
the-Fields.

On the other side of the east end of Floral Street is the whole splendid
and imposing side-length of the Opera House itself, which has its
stage-door, appropriately enough, opposite to the Nag's Head, and
its façade in Bow Street. Covent Garden Opera House is, of course,
subject for a whole book, and many a one has been written, culminating
most recently in Harold Rosenthal's sumptuous and rich volume, *Two
Centuries of Opera at Covent Garden* (1958).

In my poverty-stricken first years in London I occasionally climbed
to the Opera House's gallery—splendid to hear in if not to see from—
to experience *Die Meistersinger* (with a lovely Swedish singer, Gota
Ljunberg, as Eva), *Tristan* (with a melodious haystack of an Isolde in
Elisabeth Ohms) and a second-best *Der Rosenkavalier*. And then—when
I was still poverty-stricken, in about 1930—I was asked to a Sunday-
night dinner party in Queen Anne Street, behind the Langholm
Hotel, by a gracious lady who became my friend and patroness, Mrs
Arthur Ricketts, née Betty Wertheimer. (In parenthesis let me say
here that John Singer Sargent's glowing portraits of Betty Ricketts—
with those of her sister, her brother and her father who was Asher
Wertheimer—all wait patiently in the dark cellars of the Tate Gallery
until their brilliant painter shall return again to fashion and the daylight.) Meanwhile, some thirty years ago, at her opulent dinner-table I
sat between my hostess and her good friend the very knowledgeable
Anthony Ellis; since the talk ran on Mozart and the modern Viennese
like Lehár and Fall and Straus, they asked me to go to the opera with
them one night. I was obliged at once to raise the objection that I had
no evening clothes.

'That's an easily solved problem—you hire a dinner-suit from an emporium devoted to such purposes in the heart of Covent Garden where you live,' said Mr Ellis, and Mrs Ricketts not only took me to the emporium, and hired a dinner-suit for me to wear at the opera, but furthermore told me to keep the dinner-suit since it was a fair fit and made me look at least passable enough not to be mistaken for a waiter. The emporium, of course, was that of Moss Brothers, which will doubtless survive the Market itself.

And so I went to the Opera in proper style at last, when I was about five-and-twenty. The opera, Verdi's *Aida*; the title-role was played by Eva Turner, who had delighted me as Mascagni's Santuzza in Carl Rosa opera when I was a student at Glasgow and she was no more than a Carl Rosa soprano with a future ahead of her. All went well, and my black tie did not come undone; and in one of the intervals I was introduced to Mme Zélie de Lussan and was able to tell her that she was my very first Carmen when she sang it at Ayr with Joseph O'Mara in 1915 when I was ten. In a second interval I was introduced to Sir Arthur Pinero, who beamed under black eyebrows and bowed at me with old-fashioned courtesy; I was so stunned at an impact so dramatically overwhelming that it took me all my time to return his bow. Mrs Ricketts explained that it was my first outing and that I was very Scotch and very nervous, but that I was one day going to be a dramatic critic all the same. Mr Ellis was kind enough to add: '*And, I think, a very good one!*' A summoning bell put an end to an encounter I shall never forget. Pinero!

Further recollections of Covent Garden Opera House are no less random and no less personal. I am grateful to no less an actor than John Gielgud (later to distinguish himself at Covent Garden as director of operas by both Berlioz and Britten) for taking me to see one of the first appearances of Maria Callas in Bellini's *Norma*. (Later I was to see the same superb singer-actress in Verdi's *Traviata* at La Scala in Milan and to have a momentous luncheon with her the day after. But that is a story which belongs to my autobiography proper.)

On another happy morning I met Covent Garden's manager, Sir David Webster, walking in the vegetable market—a favourite diversion of my own—and that most genial man handed me an order which took me to the Opera House that same night to see an unusual staging of Handel's oratorio *Samson*, with the earnest advice to wait until the very end whatever I thought of static choruses. I did so, and during the last twenty minutes there glided on to the stage—like a stately

swan into a lake full of dabchicks—a new Australian soprano to sing
'Let the Bright Seraphim' with a supernatural brilliancy. It was the
now-historic first appearance on the Covent Garden stage of Miss
Joan Sutherland.

., And once—and infinitely my saddest theatrical experience of any
kind—I saw dear Kathleen Ferrier singing Gluck's *Orfeo* and making
what was to be her last appearance on any sort of stage. I met her
several times, but only in the last year of her life, and I keep a note I
had from her, acknowledging a sheaf of flowers I had sent to her on
what turned out to be her last birthday. At a supper-party in her
honour I called her to her face 'a gradely lass', and, being Lancashire-
born, she knew the meaning of the compliment. It was this heavenly
singer's ambition to sing in opera at Covent Garden, and at last three
performances of *Orfeo* were announced, though we all knew that she
was gravely ill and might not be able to fulfil her ambition. But she
did it, for two performances only, of which I saw the second and
last in the company of a dear friend, Roger Machell, who admired
Kathleen as I did. Never can the sublimely pure melodies of Gluck
have fallen upon ears more attuned. She sang nobly and serenely to
the very end of her part. But there she had reached the very end of
her resources. By a heaven-sent chance this opera concludes with a
beatific sequence of dance measures, in Gluck's most sublimely simple
style, through which Orfeo makes his or her very gradual exit into
Elysium. Her performance was completed, and she did not collapse.
It was a triumph of sheer *volonté* over physical agony. The crowd of
sister-artists instinctively clustered round her to support her off the
stage. With a similar instinct the great audience slowly left the theatre
and did not insist upon a curtain call which she could not have taken.
Only a few of those present—including my friend and I—could have
realized that she would never again make a public appearance. The
remaining performance of Gluck's *Orfeo* was quietly cancelled.

I have direct corroboration of all this in a letter from Sir John
Barbirolli: 'Yes, it was my sombre privilege to conduct both the two
performances of *Orfeo* with my beloved Kathleen Ferrier, which
brought us so close to the final tragedy. I remember going to David
Webster a year or so previously telling him of her great ambition to
sing *Orfeo* with me at the Garden and warned him that we had not
much time left in which to do it. I shall never forget his sympathy
and kindness and we got to work immediately to stage the performances.

We had scheduled three, but sadly Fate decreed there should be only two.'

Let almost the last words be those of her great friend and great critic, Sir Neville Cardus:

'The classic dignity of her art and the essentially classic "make-up"—or *Gefühl*—of her was revealed in the almost intolerably moving and bodeful performances as Orpheus (only two) which brought her career to an end, and her life, but for a few months. Seldom has Covent Garden Opera House been so beautifully solemnized as when Kathleen Ferrier flooded the place with tone which seemed as though classic shapes in marble were changing to melody, warm, rich-throated, but chaste. We who guessed the truth knew the physical pain she was enduring while she, unwittingly, was becoming a part of the immortality of Gluck, as far as this country is concerned. At the second performance, her last, pain visibly mastered her; and it was not Orpheus alone that sang "Che farò" that night but all who loved this wondrous Lancashire lass.

And finally, and still more beautifully, Sir Neville has written:

'That she was taken from us in her full rose and prime is grievous yet, nearly beyond the scope of philosophy to bear. . . . She was as brave in the face of vicissitude as she was happy in all weathers. Blow the wind southerly. She had the gift that radiates happiness. Her personal qualities even transcended her art; for great though she was as a singer, she was greater still as Kathleen Ferrier. Those of us who had the good luck and blessing to know her will never be able to separate in memory the artist in her from the warm, laughing, kind, serious, fervent, great-hearted and always uninhibitedly alive and human girl and woman that she was day in and day out, in good times or ill. Not since Ellen Terry has any artist been so universally loved.'

But we must come out of the Greek theatre and walk the surrounding streets again. Leaving the Covent Garden Opera on our right we cross Bow Street to Broad Court which runs through to Drury Lane. It is flagged, as broad as its name indicates, and for pedestrians only. It is flanked on the right by Bow Street Police Station, and on the first building on the left is a plaque or tablet at least twelve feet from the ground—too high to discern with ease or read with comfort—which has this information: 'Bow Street was formed about 1637. It has been the residence of many notable men among whom were Henry Fielding (novelist), Sir John Fielding (magistrate), Grinling Gibbons (wood-carver), Charles Macklin (actor), John Radcliffe (physician), Charles Sackville, Earl of Dorset (poet), William Wycherley (dramatist).'

To these we shall return in the next chapter when we explore Bow Street more particularly. But Broad Court itself had its great ones, too. Three famous actors of their day—Quick, Lewis, and Wroughton—all had addresses there in 1777 (the year of *The School for Scandal*). It would be pleasant to be able to record that all three were in the cast of Sheridan's blazingly successful new comedy. But none of them was—and 'facts are chiels that winna ding' (Burns's way of saying that facts have a contrary way of not fitting in with theories or with history as it ought to be). At least it may truthfully be said that John Quick had been the original Bob Acres in *The Rivals*, Sheridan's successful comedy of two years earlier, and that W. I. ('Gentleman') Lewis was the first Faulkland in the same production. He acted at Covent Garden almost continuously for thirty-six years. Of Richard Wroughton I know only that he was a useful actor who seems to have run to physical seed in his old age, for Hazlitt espied him in the course of Edmund Kean's *Richard III*, in which he played the Ghost of King Henry VI: 'Mr Wroughton makes a very substantial ghost.' He acted at Covent Garden for seventeen years, and for the rest of his long life at Drury Lane.

The little alley leading from Broad Court to Long Acre is likewise called Broad Court. It might almost be rechristened Punch Court, for it was hereabouts that there was a tavern called The Wrekin in which the celebrated *Punch: or the London Charivari* might almost be said to have been conceived. *Punch* was founded in 1841 by Henry Mayhew and Mark Lemon, the first editor. Its aims have been succinctly expressed by E. V. Knox (its editor a century later): 'Its professed purpose was to attack social abuses and the pomp and privileges of the great, but at the same time to avoid the scurrilities and improprieties which usually marked comic publications of the period. The latter stamp still remains but the radicalism of mid-Victorian satire has mellowed to a more conservative mood, largely no doubt because legislative and political reforms have gone further than the pious founders' wildest dreams.' Mark Lemon (1809–70) became the first joint-editor, then sole editor from 1843 till his death. Henry Mayhew

(1812–87), the other joint-editor, was a successful novelist and author
of the classic social survey called *London Labour and the London Poor*
(1851–62). Douglas Jerrold (1803–57), critic and wit, was a frequent
contributor to *Punch* from the start. (Moreover he lived in Broad
Court with his father as early as 1816 when he was apprentice to a
printer in Northumberland Street, Strand.) All these, together with
Henry Plunkett and Henry Baylis, authors, and Archibald Henning,
artist (three contributors to the very first number of *Punch*), used to
forgather at The Wrekin. So did the actor, Walter Lacy; Charles
Tomkins, the scene-painter of the Adelphi Theatre; the painter,
Joseph W. Allen; and Gilbert à Beckett, another *Punch* founder and
writer. All these made the welkin ring at The Wrekin!

Of this rich variety Mayhew himself has left a marvellous impression
of Covent Garden Market which is not easily abridged, though abridge
I must:

'On a Saturday—the coster's business day—it is computed that
as many as 2,000 donkey-barrows, and upwards of 3,000 women
with shallows and head-baskets visit this market during the fore-
noon.' [This appeared in 1851, and there were still a few women-
workers in the market around forty years ago. But they have nowadays almost completely vanished. The last I remember were a few
old women who shelled peas into basins just before the Second
World War.] 'About six o'clock in the morning is the best time for
viewing the wonderful restlessness of the place, for then not only is
the "Garden" itself all bustle and activity, but the buyers and
sellers stream to and from it in all directions, filling every street in
the vicinity. From Long Acre to The Strand on the one side, and
from Bow-street to Bedford-street on the other, the ground has been
seized upon by the market-goers. ... Along each approach to the
market, too, nothing is to be seen, on all sides, but vegetables; the
pavement is covered with heaps of them, waiting to be carted; the
flag-stones are stained green with the leaves trodden underfoot;
sieves and sacks full of apples and potatoes, and bundles of broccoli
and rhubarb, are left unwatched on almost every door-step; the
steps of Covent Garden Theatre are covered with fruit and vegetables; the road is blocked up with mountains of cabbages and
turnips; and men and women push past with their arms bowed out
by the cauliflowers under them, or the red tips of carrots pointing

from their crammed aprons, or else their faces are red with the weight of the loaded head-basket. [This last is also now largely done away with, and the competitive race with head-baskets piled on high is nowadays run no longer.]

'The market itself presents a beautiful scene. In the clear morning air of an autumn day the whole of the vast square is distinctly seen from one end to the other. The sky is red and golden with the newly-risen sun, and the rays falling on the fresh and vivid colours of the fruits and vegetables, brightens up the picture as with a coat of varnish. . . . Under the dark Piazza little bright dots of gas-lights are seen burning in the shops; and in the paved square the people pass and cross each other in all directions, hampers clash together, and, excepting the carters from the country, everyone is on the move. . . . Flower-girls, with large bundles of violets under their arms, run past, leaving a trail of perfume behind them. . . . Groups of apple-women, with straw pads on their crushed bonnets . . . sit on their porter's knots, chatting in Irish and smoking short pipes; every passer-by is hailed with the cry of, "Want a baskit, yer honor?" . . .

'Inside the market all is bustle and confusion. The people walk along with their eyes fixed on the goods, and frowning with thought. Men in all costumes, from the coster in his corduroy suit to the greengrocer in his blue apron, sweep past. . . . At every turn there is a fresh odour to sniff at; either the bitter aromatic perfume of the herbalists' shops breaks upon you, or the scent of oranges, then of apples, and then of onions, is caught for an instant as you move along. . . . The sieves of crimson love-apples [tomatoes] polished like china—the bundles of white glossy leeks, their roots dangling like fringe,—the celery, with its pinky stalks and bright green tops —the dark purple pickling-cabbages. . . . Then there are the apple-merchants, with their fruit of all colours, from the pale yellow green to the bright crimson, and the baskets ranged in rows on the pavement before the little shops. . . .

'Against the railings of St Paul's Church are hung baskets and slippers for sale, and near the public-house is a party of countrymen preparing their bunches of pretty coloured grass—brown and glittering, as if it had been bronzed. Between the spikes of the railings are piled up square cakes of green turf for larks; and, at the pump, boys, who have probably passed the previous night in the baskets about the market, are washing, and the water dripping from their hair that hangs in points over the face. The kerb-stone is blocked up by a crowd of admiring lads gathered round the bird-catcher's green stand, and gazing at the larks beating their breasts against their cages. . . .

'Under the Piazza the costers purchase their flowers (in pots) which they exchange in the streets for old clothes. Here is ranged a small garden of flower-pots, the musk and mignonette smelling sweetly, and the scarlet geraniums, with a perfect glow of coloured air about the flowers, standing out in rich contrast with the dark green leaves of the evergreens behind them. "There's myrtles, and larels, and boxes," says one of the men selling them, "and there's a harbora witus, and lauristiners, and that bushy shrub with pink spots is 'eath." Men and women, selling different articles, walk about under cover of the colonnade. One has seed-cake, another small-tooth and other combs, others old caps, or pig's feet, and one hawker of knives, razors, and short hatchets, may occasionally be seen driving a bargain with a countryman, who stands passing his thumb over the blade to test its keenness. Between the pillars are the coffee-stalls, with their large tin cans and piles of bread and butter . . . inside these little parlours, as it were, sit the coffee-drinkers on chairs and benches, some with a bunch of cabbages on their laps, blowing the steam from their saucers, others with their mouths full, munching away at their slices, as if not a moment could be lost. One or two porters are there besides, seated on their baskets, breakfasting with their knots on their heads.

'As you walk away from this busy scene, you meet in every street barrows and costers hurrying home. The pump in the market is now surrounded by a cluster of chattering wenches quarrelling over whose turn it is to water their drooping violets, and on the steps of Covent Garden Theatre are seated the shoeless girls, tying up the halfpenny and penny bundles.'

The scene is not all that different to this very day, though the electric lights are immeasurably brighter than naphtha flares, and the girls sitting today in Covent Garden Theatre's doorways are well-shod and not in any sense flower-girls. They are waiting—and will wait all night if necessary—to buy tickets to see the opera-star or the ballet-dancer at the height of the moment's fashion.

Let us, to conclude our examination of Long Acre, note the little street called Arne Street, near Odhams Press, which itself was on the site of what used to be the Queen's Theatre, as already described. This is the first turning on the right as we go west from Drury Lane, and in John Strype's old map of 1729 it is called Dirty Lane. A century later it became Charles Street, and it is sensibly now called after the Covent-Garden-dwelling composer whose *Masque of Alfred* contains the patriotic ditty called 'Rule Britannia'. In Butler's *Hudibras* we may find the cryptic couplet:

> He mounted Synod men, and rode 'em
> From Dirty Lane to Little Sodom.

Let us finally follow William Hazlitt (Pl. 28) in a walk along Long Acre in the other direction, elated and eloquent with the sensation of having a free pass for the theatre in his pocket. The passage is in the unfamiliar essay called *The Free Admission*, reprinted in the great essayist's 'fugitive writings' and dated 1830:

'In passing through the streets, he casts a sidelong careless glance at the playbills: he reads the papers chiefly with a view to see what is the play for the following day, or the ensuing week. If it is something new, he is glad; if it is old, he is resigned—but he goes in either case. His steps bend mechanically that way—pleasure becomes a habit, and habit a duty—he fulfils his destiny—he walks deliberately along Long Acre (you may tell a man going to the play, and whether he pays or has a free admission)—quickens his pace as he turns the corner of Bow Street, and arrives breathless and in haste at the welcome spot, where on presenting himself, he receives a passport that is a release from care, thought, toil, for the evening, and wafts him into the regions of the blest! What is it to him how the world goes round if the play goes on; whether empires rise or fall, so that Covent Garden stands its ground?... Here (by the help of that *Open Sesame!* a Free Admission), ensconced in his favourite niche, looking from the "loop-holes of retreat" in the second circle, he views the pageant of the world played before him; melts down years to moments; sees human life, like a gaudy shadow, glance across the stage; and here tastes of all earth's bliss, the sweet without the bitter, the honey without the sting, and plucks ambrosial fruits and amaranthine flowers (placed by the enchantress Fancy within his reach,) without having to pay a tax for it at the time, or repenting

of it afterwards. . . . "Oh! leave me to my repose" in my beloved
corner at Covent Garden Theatre! This (and not "the arm-chair at
an inn", though that, too, at other times, and other different
circumstances, is not without its charms,) is to me "the throne of
felicity". . . . Let me once reach and fairly establish myself in this
favourite seat, and I can bid a gay defiance to mischance, and
leave debts and duns, friends and foes, objections and arguments, far
behind me. . . . There golden thoughts unbidden betide me, and
golden visions come to me. There the dance, the laugh, the song, the
scenic deception greet me; there are wafted Shakespeare's winged
words, or Otway's plaintive lines; and there how often have I heard
young Kemble's voice, trembling at its own beauty, and prolonging
its liquid tones, like the murmur of the billowy surge on sounding
shores! . . .'

And so on and so on, with that divine afflatus which makes William
Hazlitt, even when he is word-spinning, the most heady, assured,
evocative, beguiling and sonorous of all the critics who ever genuinely
loved acting and the stage. In his London life he moved house frequently, and his lonely grave is in the churchyard of St Paul's associated
parish of St Anne's, Soho. But it is clear from such passages as that
just quoted that his heart was in Covent Garden.

Let us, finally, revert to Dirty Lane, which runs into Dryden Street
and is parallel to Drury Lane to which we are now very close. Here,
it is surmised, lived John Aubrey (1626–97). This author of the biographical repository called *Brief Lives* was in very recent years brought
back to life and fashion by a brilliant Shakespearean actor, Mr Roy
Dotrice, in a one-man entertainment of the same title, *Brief Lives*,
which kept the Criterion Theatre packed for months and months. The
actor, himself impersonating the quaint old codger and antiquary,
gave him a kind of Rabelaisian virtuosity as well as a continuous
charm, the rare quality of incalculability in both speech and action,
and an occasional deep pathos. Whether he lived in Covent Garden
or not—and the actor appropriately placed him in Dirty Lane off
Drury Lane—Aubrey certainly knew several Covent Garden worthies.

For example he knew Sir William Davenant (1606–68) who claimed
to be an Oxford-born bastard son of William Shakespeare himself. He
tells us that Davenant served as page to the first Duchess of Richmond,
and later as manservant to that singular spark of genius, Fulke Greville,

before becoming a writer of masques and a theatre-manager when the theatres reopened. Then suddenly Aubrey, in his startlingly abrupt fashion, tells us of Davenant: 'He gott a terrible Clap of a black handsome wench that lay in Axe-Yard, Westminster . . . which cost him his nose, with which unlucky mischance many Witts were too cruelly bold. . . .'

Aubrey also knew and tells us a little about Sir Kenelm Digby (1603–65), who was one of the many tenants of that great and still extant house in King Street in which we shall linger at the very end of our tour. Also of Sir Kenelm's beautiful wife who had been Venetia Stanley and who had been painted more than once by Sir Anthony Van Dyck himself. Sir Kenelm's father, Sir Everard, had been hanged for his participation in the Gunpowder Plot, and he had other connections, qualities and attributes. But his physique would seem to have been old Aubrey's principal concern: 'He was such a goodly handsome Person, gigantique and of great Voice.' But then old Aubrey was almost too susceptible to manly beauty. In exactly sixty words he gives a pen-picture of the Cavalier poet Richard Lovelace (1618–58), whose poetry in general has been declared 'slovenly and insipid' though he wrote two inspired and perfect short lyrics, one to Althea and one to Lucasta, which keep his name—like Edmund Waller's—deathless in the anthologies. Aubrey was more interested in the person than in the poet:

'Richard Lovelace, Esq.; he was a most beautifull gentleman.

'Obiit in a cellar in Long Acre, a little before the restauration of his Majestie. Mr Edmund Wyld, etc, have made collections for him, and given him money.

'One of the handsomest men in England. He was an extraordinary handsome man, but prowd. He wrote a Poem called *Lucasta*.'

CHAPTER FOUR

BITTERSWEET OLD DRURY

Sir Richard Steele (Pl. 16), who loved and haunted Covent Garden as much as most others of its legion of worthies, has this about Drury Lane in one of his *Tatler* essays (26th July 1709):

'There is near Covent Garden a street known by the name of Drury, which before the days of Christianity was purchased by the Queen of Paphos, and is the only part of Great Britain where the tenure of vassalage is still in being. All that long course of buildings is under particular districts, or ladyships, after the manner of lordships in other parts, over which matrons of known abilities preside and have, for the support of their age and infirmities, certain taxes paid out of the rewards of the amorous labours of the young. This seraglio of Great Britain is disposed into convenient alleys and apartments, and every house from the cellar to the garret is inhabited by nymphs of different orders, that persons of every rank may be accommodated.'

Behind Steele's elegant screen of periphrasis we may easily discern the plain, ungarnished and indeed ungarnishable fact that Drury Lane—when Queen Anne was alive—was a hotbed of hot beds, a congeries of brothels and stews, no longer even pretending to be the bagnios and hummums and semi-public baths whose sites we have already visited in Long Acre and the Piazza. This Old Drury had a dense population of whores young and old, pimps and punks, panders and procuresses, all of them kept lively and prosperous (when well enough to receive visitors in their rackety rooms) by a motley variety of insatiable customers ranging from more or less noble lords to the ignoblest of their varlets and satellites and toadies. And all this bargaining and choosing and arranging, squabbling and complying, was conducted and misconducted in a thick miasma compounded in equal parts of noisome stink and cheap lavender water. The scene and the conditions were pretty much the same for at least one hundred and fifty years after Queen Anne was dead.

Drury Lane is a very ancient and quite narrow thoroughfare running north and south, from St Giles to what is now the Aldwych. It took its name from Sir Thomas Drury who owned Drury House at the latter or Strand end. This was at the point where Kingsway now enters Aldwych, a little to the north of the imposing front portals of Bush House. An old name for Drury Lane, though one not often used, was Via de Aldwych. The latter word is said to be of Danish origin. Throughout the hundred years before Queen Anne came to the throne Drury Lane was aristocratic and had many stately residences. Soon after the accession of William and Mary it rapidly degenerated. But in the previous century many noblemen, men of letters and actors, and aristocratic poets like Sir William Alexander, Earl of Stirling, dwelt in Drury Lane. The latter was Secretary of State for Scotland under King James I. It has been justly said of his long-winded verse: 'There is less of conceit in the merely conceitful sense than was common with contemporaries, and if you only persevere, opalescent hues edge long passages otherwise comparable with mist and fog.' John Lacy, perhaps the best-known of the old actors who lived in Old Drury, was an original member of the King's Company (Thomas Killigrew's) and remained with it till his death in 1684. He was always a favourite actor of Pepys and Evelyn, the diarists. His great part was Bayes in George Villiers's comedy *The Rehearsal*, a part which he originated. He died in his house in Drury Lane, 'two doors off Lord Anglesey's house', and near Cradle Alley, and was buried in the farther churchyard of St Martin-in-the-Fields. Lacy is said to have given lessons to Nell Gwynne (Pl. 11) and to have been one of her lovers. She too lived in Drury Lane, and her birthplace may have been in Coal Yard just off it (if it was not in the city of Hereford). Her mother was buried in St Martin-in-the-Fields and Nell in due course shared her grave. She appears to have been only thirty-seven when she died in 1687, but the short life was a merry one since she was the mistress not only of the actors Hart and Lacy but also of King Charles II.

One of the pleasantest real-life glimpses we get of her is in Pepys's account of seeing 'pretty Nelly standing at her lodgings in Drury Lane in her smock-sleeves and bodice' and watching the May Day revels. The critic Joseph Knight, writing long afterwards, said of her with some pomposity: 'Innumerable stories, many of them diverting and all of them unedifying, are transmitted by tradition, and contain no inherent improbability.' Mme de Sévigné, her French contemporary, says of Nell Gwynne in a letter: 'She is young, indiscreet, confident, wild, and of an agreeable humour; she sings, she dances, she acts her part with a good grace. She has a son by the king and hopes to have him acknowledged.' Strictly I have perhaps no business to pursue this eminently pursuable creature, since her lodgings were probably in the north end of Drury Lane, and this book's province is, strictly or loosely, only the south side, i.e. from Long Acre to The Strand; but it is difficult to leave the subject of 'pretty witty Nell' just because she lived in the wrong part of Drury Lane. After all, she plied her trade in the theatres, which *are* within my province.

Clifford Bax, who wrote the best of all the books about her, caught her significance on his very first page: 'No one can think of her without a kindling of kindness; nor would it be too much to say that, although she has been dead for two hundred and fifty years [now nearer three hundred], men still fall in love with her. That is the fate of exceedingly few women—perhaps of not more than five or six. Nell Gwynn, in fact, has been one of the darlings of Destiny.' And within the same paragraph the same writer observes: 'To those who are born to speak English her name has more sunlight in it than the name of any other woman in history.' For to history she belongs, as distinct from stage history. Not only did she become one of the many mistresses of King Charles II; she also bore him a son who became Duke of St Albans and was seventeen when his mother died. His career was military and honourable and he ended up as Lord Lieutenant of Berkshire under King George I. In her will she desired that she should be buried in St Martin-in-the-Fields and she was so. She also desired that Dr Tenison, later to become Archbishop of Canterbury, might preach her funeral sermon, and he did so. She bequeathed to the same church 'a decent pulpit-cloth and cushion', and in her will and its two codicils she showed many instances of her gratitude to friends and servants and the London poor.

The Notebook of an anonymous theatre manager records: 'She was low in stature, and what the French call *mignonne* and *piquante*, well-formed, handsome, but red-haired, and rather *embonpoint* . . . she had remarkably lively eyes, but so small they were almost invisible when she laughed; and a foot, the least of any women in England.' More than a century after her death, Leigh Hunt, England's first major drama critic, gives a description of what she was 'like', doubtless culled and digested from many such reliable reminiscences: 'This celebrated actress, who was as excellent in certain giddy parts of comedy as she was inferior in tragedy, was small of person, but very pretty, with a good-humoured face, and eyes that winked when she laughed.'

Another remarkable character who seems never to have been able to stay long away from Covent Garden was Colley Cibber's second daughter, Charlotte. She kept a questionable tavern in Drury Lane and died around 1760. She has told the curious all about herself in a volume, now rare, entitled *The Life of Charlotte Charke by Herself* (1755). She is by no means unwitty and calls the little book 'some account of my unaccountable life'. She arrived belated into Cibber's family—his last born—as a kind of black ewe, and Cibber himself had as little as possible to do with her. But he could not keep her off the stage. She loved masculine clothes and played male parts much oftener than female. This was for the most part in touring companies, and she seems to have communicated with her family only to borrow money. She had married when still very young a violinist at Drury Lane called Richard Charke, but she did not stay long by his side, nor he by hers. She is frank and racy about her marriage as about most other things in her life:

'As I have, among many other Censures, laboured under that of being a giddy, indiscreet Wife, I must take this Opportunity of referring myself to the superior Judgment of those who read my Story; whether a young Creature, who actually married for Love, must not naturally be incensed, when, in less than a Month after Marriage, I received the most demonstrative Proofs of Disregard, where I ought to have found the greatest Tenderness. To be even to my Face apparently convinced of his insatiable Fondness for a Plurality of common Wretches, that were to be had for Half a Crown!'

Leaving her husband to those very cheap devices Mrs Charke tried to set up a respectable business: 'I took it into my Head to dive into TRADE. To that End, I took a Shop in Long Acre, and turned Oil Woman and Grocer.' This did not last long: 'I think in about three months after, I positively threw it up, at a Hundred Pounds Stock, all paid for, to keep a grand Puppet Show over the Tennis Court in James Street, which is licensed. . . .' The estranged husband, meanwhile, was occasionally on the doorstep, and I give a little more of her account since it illustrates her pungent style as well as it conveys 'the tone of the time' and the savour of the place:

'I knew that he had a Right to make bold with any Thing that was mine, as there was no formal Article of Separation between us. And I could not easily brook his taking any Thing from me to be so profusely expended on his Mistress, who lived no farther from me than the House next to the Coach-Maker's in Great Queen's Street, and was Sister to the famous Mrs Sally King, one of the Ladies of the HIGHEST IRREPUTABLE REPUTATION at that Time, in or about Covent Garden. However, to prevent any Danger, I gave and took all Receipts (till Mr Charke went to Jamaica, where he died in about twenty Months after his leaving England) in the Name of a Widow Gentlewoman, who boarded with me, and I sat quiet and snug with the pleasing Reflection of my Security. . . .'

Mrs Charke strenuously denies various rumours about her occupations and habits, especially one about her having hurled a fish at her distinguished father, who obviously found her existence an embarrassment:

'Upon being met with a Hare in my Hand, carried by Order to the Peer I then lately lived with, this single Creature was enumerated into a long Pole of Rabbits; and 'twas affirmed as a Truth that I made it my daily Practice to cry them about the Streets.
'This Falsehood was succeeded by another, that of my selling Fish, an Article I never thought of dealing in; but notwithstanding, the wicked Forger of this Story positively declared that I was selling some Flounders one Day, and seeing my Father, stepped most audaciously up to him, and slapt one of the largest I had full in his Face. Who, that has common Senses, could be so credulous to receive the least Impression from so inconsistent a Tale; or that, if it had been true, if I had escaped my Father's Rage, the Mob would not, with strictest Justice, have prevented my surviving such an unparalleled Villainy one Moment?'

Charlotte's denials, in short, ring untrue; and she was obviously too shrewd a beldame not to know that the best way to publicize a rumour is to deny it. She ended her days obscurely, but spent some at least of her later years in Drury Lane keeping a tavern which was of ill repute when she took it over, and whose character she may, or may not, have repaired:

'I soon grew tired of leading such a Life of Fear, and resolved to make Trial of the Friendship of my late Uncle, and wrote a melancholy Epistle to him; earnestly imploring his Assistance, for the sake of his deceased Sister (my dear Mother) to give me as much money as would be necessary to set me up in a Publick House. I told him, I would not put it upon the Foot of borrowing, as 'twas ten Millions to one whether he might ever be repaid; and, in Case of Failure of a Promise of that Nature, I knew I must of course be subject to his Displeasure, therefore fairly desired him to make it a Gift, if he thought my Circumstances worth his Consideration; which, to do him Justice, indeed he did, and ordered me to take a House directly, that he might be assured of the Sincerity of my Intention.

'I obeyed his Commands the next Day, and, as I have been in a Hurry from the Hour of my Birth, precipitately took the first House where I saw a Bill, and which, unfortunately for me, was in Drury Lane, that had been most irregularly and indecently kept by the last Incumbent, who was a celebrated Dealer in murdered Reputations, Wholesale and Retail.'

Dekker and Middleton fifty years earlier might have had a prevision of Charlotte Charke when they called a play of theirs *The Roaring Girl*.

Very much more recent inhabitants of Drury Lane have been the actor Charles Laughton and the conductor Sir John Barbirolli. Laughton I knew and first met even before he first leapt into fame. I came face to face with him one day in Long Acre when he was rehearsing the part of Mr Pickwick (for an unsuccessful stage production at the Haymarket). I asked him if he was exploring the Market and he said: 'Not at all, my dear fellow. I live round the corner in Drury Lane above a chemist's shop.' He was in lodgings there for several weeks near the corner of Long Acre and Drury Lane, and he told me a little about his landlady who was 'purest Dickens'. As always, Laughton struck me as a man oozing with genius.

The connection of the great conductor with this unlikely street was, at first, more a matter of hearsay. I wrote to him (not long before his sudden death in 1970) asking for confirmation or denial of the rumour that he was the son of an Italian musician and was actually born in Drury Lane, and, if so, at what number. He answered with his characteristic prompt politeness:

'As regards my birthplace, I was not born in Drury Lane, although I was taken to live there when I was two, and remained until I was seven. (The chemist's shop to which you refer I remember very well indeed.) No. 37 Drury Lane is now in exactly the same condition as when I went there, except that the ground floor shop now specializes in fine coffees and Italian wines. . . . I was actually born in Southampton Row over a baker's shop in which my father and mother had lodgings, and the exact site of it is now the Grand Hotel, at the top of that little alley-way [Cosmo Place] which leads to Queen Square where the Italian Hospital is situated. It is a very strange coincidence that one side of the hospital is in a street [Boswell Street] whose name I cannot for the moment remember, where my father found lodgings when he first arrived in London in 1893 to take up an engagement in the orchestra of the Savoy Hotel, and that he died in the Italian Hospital in the same street in which he had first lodged.'

Long Acre divides upper from lower Drury Lane. It is continued to the east side in Great Queen Street, into which we must penetrate a few yards—just as far as the huge Masonic Temple built in the second decade of the present century. This, though it has its many detractors, has always seemed to me a not ignoble building which doubtless fulfils its function admirably. But it has a black mark on its character. While researching into the ramifications of the sale of the Covent Garden Estate I came—by as pretty a piece of serendipity as any in my experience as a regular serendipitist—upon a drawing and a story in the files of the *Manchester Guardian* for the same year of the sale, 1913. Serendipity—need I explain?—is the happy discovery of one thing when looking for something quite other.

Turning the pages for the end of 1913—and the end of my day's searching—I suddenly came upon an arresting drawing (Pl. 15) in the issue of Saturday, 20th December, with the heading ,'The Effort to Preserve a House where Boswell Lived'. The drawing was signed

'Frank L. Emanuel' and dated 17–12–13, and beneath it was an utterly beguiling note, simply initialled 'P' and speaking for itself:

'Boswell's house in Great Queen Street, whose beetling cornice breaks the roof line so pleasantly, will be pulled down unless the authorities of Freemasons' Hall relent. The space is wanted for an extension to the hall. The Society for the Preservation of Ancient Buildings is pleading for the life of the house, and especially for its fine classical front. The Society suggests that even if the house must go the front and the roof, with its five staggering dormer windows, might be preserved, and offers to give professional services in supervising the necessary work of repair. There ought to be little difficulty in raising the money needed by public subscription. It is rather surprising that the Freemasons, with their traditional connection with building, should propose to destroy one of the best examples in London of Renaissance house building. The house— there was originally one house only, although it was divided into two certainly before Boswell went to live either in No. 55 or No. 56; the point is still in dispute—is by far the most distinguished in a street full of memories of the great eighteenth-century times. The chief architectural interest of the house is the tradition which says that it was built either from the designs of Inigo Jones or those of his pupil Webbe. The peculiar spreading character of the Corinthian capitals is said by experts to be a characteristic of Inigo Jones. It is certain from old prints that the house is the only survivor of the stately row. Three firms now nest in different parts of the large old-fashioned "mansion," as it is called by "Perdita" Robinson, who by tradition once lived in it. The rooms are panelled throughout, as the Society has discovered by probing underneath the canvas and wallpaper.

'The dispute as to whether No. 55 or No. 56 was the house Boswell lived in for several years while he was writing the great Life is of no importance with regard to the effort for preservation. There is no question of preserving one and not the other. The London County Council plaque was placed on No. 56 in 1905 as the result of the pioneer research work by Sir Laurence Gomme, who identified this as the house from the evidence of the parish rate-books. Mr. Christian Tearle has just unearthed new evidence from the Law List, which shows that Boswell lived next door. If so, he lived in much the better half, and he had a noble staircase to enter by, instead of a commonplace flight. None of his biographers knew where he lived in the street, including Sir Leslie Stephen, who wrote the life in the National Dictionary of Biography. Boswell took the house in 1786, or perhaps a year or two later. His friend Hoole, the translator of Ariosto and Tasso, had lived there before him. Johnson had died in 1784, and Boswell was deep in his great book. Sir Laurence Gomme thinks that he wrote the chapters covering the last seven years of Johnson's life in the Great Queen Street house. There is an interesting letter which Boswell wrote at this time to Bishop Percy, asking for anecdotes of Johnson, and explaining his method of biography. He says characteristically: "It appears to me that mine is the best plan of biography that can be conceived for my readers will as near as may be accompany Johnson in his progress. . . . It is wonderful what avidity there still is for everything relative to Johnson." Boswell after Johnson's death fell as we know upon melancholy times, and there is a curious self-revelatory letter to his friend Temple written almost certainly from Great Queen Street in 1788, in which he says—"I have been wretchedly dissipated, so that I have not written a line for a fortnight, but to-day I shall resume my pen, and shall labour vigorously. Am now in strong, steady spirits. P.S.: My wife is, I thank God, much better. But is it not a crime to keep her in this pernicious air, when she might be so much better at Auchinleck?" In the following year Mrs Boswell returned to the pure air of Auchinleck, leaving Boswell alone, and he tells a friend that his wife had written recommending him to "take a house in a well-aired situation." So he left Great Queen Street, and took a house in Queen Anne Street, Cavendish Square, "very small, but neat." By this time the "rough draught" of the Life was finished. He died in 1795 in a Great Portland Street house which was pulled down long ago. Boswell had always, in his own words, "as violent an affection" for London "as the most romantic lover ever had for his mistress". Nearly all the evidences of his restless roamings have gone but this Great Queen Street house, and all who love his name (and who does not?) are anxious lest this, too, should disappear.'

Peabody Buildings, examples of which are plentiful in the Market, in lower Drury Lane and in Bedfordbury particularly, began in

Spitalfields in 1864 and spread to Chelsea, Bermondsey, Islington and to Covent Garden. More than one porter of my acquaintance was born and had spent all his days in a Peabody flat. 'Nothink much wrong with the old Peabody Building', said one to me, though he agreed that the prison-like style of their exteriors is not exactly a thing of beauty. 'They now have bathrooms—for them as wants 'em!'

Peabody Buildings are huge, condensed, mean-looking dwellings for the poor—unhappy-looking homes for doubtless happy families. We meet them round the corner again in Wild Street, and yet again in Bedford-bury. Those in Drury Lane cover the site of the old Cockpit Theatre.

They were all of them endowed by the American philanthropist George Peabody (1795–1869), whose ancestors went from Leicester to New England in 1635. The source of the Peabody wealth was a series of dry-goods stores which were 'all over the place' like the subsequent Peabody Buildings. He withdrew from his business concerns in 1843 to go to London and become a banker. He died in the year 1869 in the house of a friend in Eaton Square, and it is furthermore curious to note that his body lay for a month in Westminster Abbey before being shipped for burial in his native town of Danvers, Mass. Peabody was a genuinely charitable and unambitious man: he refused a baronetcy in England. His name is honoured as a promoter of Anglo-American friendship and understanding. His gifts to Harvard and Yale, to the cause of Negro education and to the well-being and adequate housing of the London poor were prodigious. But his money did not inspire good-looking architecture.

Of the surviving features of the lower part of Drury Lane, the only notable one is the Aldwych Theatre whose front entrance is at the corner where it runs into the Aldwych semi-circle. This and the similarly constructed Strand Theatre occupy two corners of a big quadrilateral block in the Aldwych, between Drury Lane and Catherine Street and with Tavistock Street in the rear. The two theatres had identical façades and very similar interiors, and between them is a large hotel, the Waldorf, which was not built until both the theatres were opened. These changes were only a tiny part of an immense slum-demolition scheme and reconstruction of the whole neighbour-hood which began in the middle of the nineteenth century and cul-minated in the building of Bush House, that stately and capacious monument to Anglo-American relations.

The Aldwych Theatre was opened in time for Christmas 1905 with *Bluebell*, a new edition of Seymour Hicks's *Bluebell in Fairyland* with Hicks's charming wife Ellaline Terriss as its star. The theatre had been built by Hicks in collaboration with his manager, the great Charles Frohman. The opening show had been promoted from the Vaudeville Theatre, and Miss Terriss herself described it in her reminiscences: 'This beautiful story of London—and The Strand and Drury Lane— and then Dreamland or Fairyland, whichever you choose to make it, was written by Seymour Hicks and Walter Slaughter (who did the music). The children loved it and I am not at all sure that the grown-up children did not love it more. It told the story of a little crossing-sweeper, Dicky—which Seymour played—and a little flower girl, Bluebell—which was me. . . .' And later on she gives an instance of the shrewdness that lay behind all that charm of hers: 'We did this revival for several reasons—because this was a popular play for Christmas, and also because it is never easy to get the public to come to a newly opened theatre. But with such an attraction as *Bluebell* we knew they would come, find out where it was—and they did.' In December 1965 the London Theatre Museum in Holland Park had an Aldwych Theatre exhibition to celebrate the theatre's sixtieth birthday, and there declaring it open—scorning a chair, erect as a ramrod, and with a voice as clear as a bell—was the sweet old Ellaline Terriss, charming as ever, and at the incredible age of ninety-three. She reached the great age of 100, shortly before her death in 1971.

To myself the most memorable productions at the Aldwych Theatre were both American plays—Lillian Hellman's *Watch on the Rhine* in 1942, an extraordinarily moving piece in which a likeable little German family fled from Nazidom to a gracious and elegant house in Washington; and Tennessee Williams's *Streetcar Named Desire* in 1949, in which Vivien Leigh, by that time my very dear friend, gave perhaps the most intense of all her performances. But long before these there was the long régime of the Aldwych farces—many of them by Ben Travers, and most of them containing such delectable comedians as Tom Walls, Ralph Lynn and Robertson Hare. And after all these things the Aldwych has become the London headquarters of the Royal Shakespeare Theatre of Stratford-on-Avon, the two together making a formidable friendly rival to the Old Vic-cum-National Theatre on the opposite side of the Thames. This concatenation is—and must be—a little puzzling to European and other foreign visitors of culture who stop one in The Strand to ask the whereabouts of the Shakespeare Theatre situated at something that sounds like Alt Week, and may either be the Old Vic or the Aldwych!

Since the Stratford-on-Avon company took over the Aldwych Theatre, playgoers have had many rewarding experiences, especially when the company included Paul Scofield or Peggy Ashcroft. My oddest visit was to the morbid play called *Marat-Sade* whose action is set entirely in a late eighteenth-century lunatic asylum in France. It was a matinee, and there was not a soul I knew in the crowded audience, which was of the weirdly dressed, ultra-modern sort, mainly young, the boys' hair being as long as if not longer than that of the girls. I was not too well in health, just recovering from some cortisone treatment for eye-trouble, a treatment to which I proved utterly allergic. And at the interval, feeling thus unlike myself, I wandered into the foyer and, suddenly looking up, I saw all the faces of the playgoers in the smokers' gallery looking down at me with what I imagined to be broad-grinning amusement. 'Am I going mad myself?' I asked myself, and I staggered along the curved lobby that leads back to the auditorium. Suddenly I was confronted in the lobby with a stage-photo of Gaev tenderly embracing his sister Mme Ranevsky in a recent revival, of course at this same theatre, of Chekhov's *The Cherry Orchard*. And I returned to tranquillity and complete sanity with the reflection: 'But I am sane, and this is sane theatre as I understand and love it. This is sanity, thank Heaven!' The players so charmingly, so salutarily portrayed were John Gielgud and Peggy Ashcroft. I thanked them the next time I met them together.

The Strand Theatre, at the Catherine-street end of the same block, opened in 1905 as the Waldorf Theatre, and changed its name again to the Whitney Theatre before it finally became The Strand. It opened extraordinarily with a touring Italian opera company, the operas being interrupted by appearances of the sublime Italian actress, Eleonora Duse (Pl. 32), then at the height of her long heyday. Her first performance at the Waldorf was in an Italian translation of Pinero's *The Second Mrs. Tanqueray*. This was called in Italian simply *La Seconda Moglie* (or *The Second Wife*), and it was not a part that particularly suited Duse's ineffable style. Mrs Tanqueray was, so to speak, *effable*, and the original Mrs Patrick Campbell clearly played her so in her triumphant performance. She went to see Duse, of course, and comments astutely and without envy or malice: 'To me she is too sad, and too slow. But in her work there is a great dignity, sincerity, a fine introspection—and a tremendous appreciation of the nobility of suffering. . . . The Madonna-like atmosphere of her personality eclipses sometimes the charm of her sincerity in modern neurotic roles.' A Madonna-like Paula Tanqueray is a contradiction in terms, an oxymoron. Mrs Campbell knew it, and said so. The best critic of her day, A. B. Walkley, said it just as well but no better: 'One does not care to see a great virtuosa performing on a cottage piano. Was Paula, the ex-Mrs. Jarman, really so splendid, so romantic a figure as this? I cannot believe it. . . . This is no Mrs. Tanqueray, who "adores fruit, especially when it is expensive", but an exquisite orchidaceous creature with the enigmatic smile of a Da Vinci portrait and tones in her voice that are echoed from a Stradivarius. It is not Paula fondling and caressing Aubrey, but some Vivien beguiling Merlin. In a word Signora Duse inevitably poetises the prose of the play, and so warps it from its real nature. . . .'

In *La Locandiera* of Goldoni, which was Duse's second play at the Waldorf, all was well again and all was smiles. Walkley capitulates and surrenders, and gives the performance the highest praise in his critical power: 'Night after night, year after year, I have gone to theatre after theatre, and, though I have not found all barren, yet on the whole I should be inclined to sigh over a misspent life were it not for the thought of Duse in *La Locandiera*. For the sake of that one supreme pleasure I might be tempted to go through it all again. . . .' A rather favourable notice!

In its first years the Strand Theatre had no particular prosperity till along came Matheson Lang in 1913 with *Mr. Wu*, which ran for a year. Between the wars—from 1919 to 1923—the theatre was under the actor-managership of Arthur Bourchier, an actor forceful rather than great, who played the congenial part of Long John Silver every Christmas during his tenancy, until 1926 in fact. The theatre, like the Aldwych, also had its prolonged farcical phase with Leslie Henson, Alfred Drayton and Robertson Hare fooling themselves to the top of their bent. At this theatre in the Second World War Donald Wolfit staged a daily hour of Shakespeare in the darkest and noisiest days of the world conflict. The scheme was called 'Lunch-Time Shakespeare', and one particularly recalls scenes from *The Merry Wives* with Wolfit as Falstaff and the Vanbrugh Sisters as Mistress Ford and Mistress Page killing themselves with laughter and with the well-concealed strain of remembering unfamiliar lines. Wolfit also had the splendid temerity to revive here John Ford's tragedy of brother-sister incest, '*Tis Pity She's a Whore*. I remember asking two French sailors in the audience what they might call this play in France, and one answered immediately and with a grin: 'Sans doute, *C'est Dommage que c'est une Cocotte!*'

Commentators on London often overlook the fact that this neighbourhood of Strand and Aldwych is quite as much part of London's theatre-land as is Shaftesbury Avenue. In Catherine Street itself is the newish Duchess Theatre and the Theatre Royal, Drury Lane, itself with its incomparable history; and further down The Strand are the Vaudeville and the Adelphi. There is also the relic of the celebrated Lyceum. Moreover there are hereabouts many vanished theatres with no relics or traces to show. A previous Strand Theatre—known as the Royal Strand—existed until 1906 in The Strand itself, where the Aldwych Tube station is now situated. Never do I pass or enter this station without recalling that here from the beginning of the nineteenth century stood a theatre that housed panoramas; that in 1832 a famous Yorkshire comedian rechristened it Rayner's New Subscription Theatre in The Strand; that in 1836 it was put on the same footing as the Olympic and Adelphi Theatres and staged several of Dickens's novels in dramatic form; that from 1848 till 1850 it was under the command of one of the innumerable William Farrens; and that in 1901, after many ups-and-downs involving Mrs Keeley, Mrs Stirling (Pl. 22), and Marie Wilton (later Lady Bancroft), it housed a musical comedy called *A Chinese Honeymoon* which had a then-record run of 1,075 performances and has, oddly enough, never had a major revival, even though its lilting music was by Howard Talbot (who was later to collaborate with both Paul Rubens and Lionel Monckton in pieces whose tunes linger with us still).

The original Gaiety was on a site on the opposite side of the way with an entrance in The Strand (now Aldwych), a pit and gallery entrance in Catherine Street, and a stage-door in Wellington Street. This original Gaiety had been built on the site of the Strand Music Hall by Lionel Lawson of the *Daily Telegraph*; a restaurant was incorporated into the new building. The manager who opened this theatre and made it famous was John Hollingshead (Pl. 26), of whom more in chapter five. He was at first unlucky. Fire broke out and very nearly delayed the opening. The workmen still in the building insisted on remaining there to see the first performance. In his company were Alfred Wigan, Madge Robertson (later Mrs Kendal) and Nelly Farren (Pl. 27), a pocket genius of whom a critic was to write: 'Miss Farren may be a wife and a mother, but she is certainly one of the best boys in existence.' Charles Dickens in 1870 saw what must have been one of the last plays he was to see in this or any other theatre. It was a drama by H. J. Byron called *Uncle Dick's Darling*, and Dickens beheld in it the young actor called Henry Irving for whom he had already prophesied a great career.

The journalist Edmund Yates wrote the following letter to Irving dated Good Friday, 1870:

'My dear Irving, I think you would like to know that when I was dining with Mr. Charles Dickens the other day, he spoke in very high terms of your performance in *Uncle Dick's Darling*. He seemed especially struck with your earnestness and your never forgetting to elaborate, even by small detail, your conception and study of the character. He said, too, that more than once, you reminded him strongly of my father, and I know that, from Mr Dickens, it is meant as very high praise.'

The elder Yates, of whom Irving reminded Dickens, was a good useful actor who died in 1842 and who had in his time played Iago to Young's Othello, Falstaff to Macready's Hotspur, and Fagin, Mr Mantalini and Miss Miggs in dramatizations of Dickens's own novels.

But it was Nelly Farren who was the particular genius of the old Gaiety and its celebrated Burlesques. That venerable charmer and exemplary autobiographer Graham Robertson (whom I was proud to call my friend in his extreme old age) has reminisced delectably about Nelly Farren:

'Her name sounds to me like a laugh—the echo of many delightful laughs. I suppose it is now necessary to state that Nelly Farren was what was then called a Burlesque Actress and was Principal Boy at the Gaiety Theatre. The Gaiety Burlesques were not achievements to be remembered with pride; puns stood for wit, jingling rhyme carried along dull dialogue, the productions were upon the ordinary pantomime lines, and the costumes quite peculiarly ugly.

But—they gave us Nelly Farren. Kate Vaughan, the exquisite, floated through them, vaporous, dreamlike; Edward Terry, grotesque as a Gothic gargoyle, had a quaint and original comic force. But it was the genius of Nelly Farren that held together those feeble extravaganzas, and when she left the stage it became at once clear that they were beyond human endurance. But Nelly seemed pleased enough with them; content to make pleasant little bricks without a particle of straw; to lend wit and sparkle to dull lines by her humour and charm. After all, she was doing something that nobody else could do, and that must always be amusing. . . . Towards the end of Miss Farren's reign, a change had come over the Gaiety burlesque, showing a certain falling off in fun and in all-round acting, but a decided gain in beauty. Fred Leslie, a comedian of peculiar charm, replaced Edward Terry, Sylvia Grey succeeded Kate Vaughan the peerless, but avoided comparison by her originality and girlish freshness: she was an exquisite dancer. Nelly Farren alone remained unchanged; in no way did her natural force abate.'

To the old Gaiety when near its last days George Edwardes transferred a show called *In Town*, which began its run in 1892 and is usually regarded as the very first musical comedy as we know the *genre* to this day—a show with more sentiment and less irony than the old burlesque, of which it may be said to have been a development of a sort. The last show at the old Gaiety before it was re-built over the way was a musical comedy called *The Toreador*, which had music by Ivan Caryll and Lionel Monckton and a book by J. T. Tanner (part-author of *In Town*) and Harry Nicholls. Its chief star was a brand-newcomer called Gertie Millar, making her first London appearance. Her first-appearance-ever had been as girl-babe in a Manchester pantomime of *Babes in the Wood* in 1892. She had piquancy, lightness and grace, and, rather than being lovely or even pretty, she had *la petite frimousse éveillée* that was the great Réjane's attribute, 'the wideawake little phiz'. These qualities, greatly aided by a small but excellent singing voice, kept Gertie Millar a great public favourite until her marriage to the Earl of Dudley. She had previously been happily married to the composer Lionel Monckton, who died in 1924. She 'retired into the ranks of the aristocracy' on the occasion of her second marriage. It was Gertie Millar who opened the second Gaiety just as she had closed the first. And she reigned for seven years at the handsome new theatre, beginning in *The Orchid*, the play being wholly by J. T. Tanner and the music once again by Ivan Caryll and Lionel Monckton. *The Times* (27th October 1903) had this comment:

'If any hopes had been formed that a new house would mean a new policy, *The Orchid* will disappoint them. The Gaiety is very consistent. We critics may ask it to be witty—to be poetic, Aristophanic, to show us our social hypocrisies in the clear light of laughter, to hold us up to our own ridicule. But this theatre can be imagined as answering: "What's Aristophanes to me? I don't want to make you think. I am inconsequent, irresponsible, irrelevant; I know it, but just see what a lot of pretty girls I've got!"

'The kaleidoscope of *The Orchid* is as gay as any of its predecessors. . . . There is no denying that now and then the chorus at the old Gaiety was a little too languidly beautiful to be quite entertaining; the chorus at the new Gaiety is quite as beautiful and full of high spirits. . . . A dance of boys in white, with Miss Gertie Millar to shepherd them, is a very dainty conception. Here also were Mr. Edmund Payne, Mr. George Grossmith, Jun., and Miss Connie Ediss as her inimitable self.'

This was in 1903, and the theatre stayed open until 1938 when it became a shell, empty and dark, until after the war when it was demolished to be replaced by television offices. Someone had the sensibility to place a plaque on the new building on The Strand side. It reads— although very few busy passers-by stop to read it—as follows:

ON THIS SITE
STOOD THE GAIETY THEATRE
BUILT IN 1903 FOR
IMPRESARIO GEORGE EDWARDES
THE THEATRE OPENED
WITH THE PERFORMANCE OF
'THE ORCHID' AND UNTIL IT
WAS CLOSED IN 1938 REMAINED
THE HOME OF MUSICAL COMEDY
AND ONE OF LONDON'S MOST
FAMOUS PLAYHOUSES

Two or three yards away—on the wall of Marconi House—is another plaque which gets similarly passed by and unread, for the most part. Yet it is just as explicit and just as deeply interesting—it may even be said to be, in a sense, of world-wide interest:

WITHIN THIS BUILDING
MARCONI'S WIRELESS
TELEGRAPH COMPANY
LTD. OPERATED THEIR
FAMOUS BROADCASTING
STATION 2.L.O. FROM MAY
IITH TO NOVEMBER 15TH
1922 WHEN IT BECAME
THE FIRST STATION OF THE
BRITISH BROADCASTING
COMPANY

THE FIRST PRE-ANNOUNCED BROADCAST
OF PUBLIC ENTERTAINMENT IN THE
WORLD TOOK PLACE TWO YEARS
EARLIER WHEN DAME NELLIE MELBA
SANG FROM MARCONI'S CHELMSFORD
WORKS ON JUNE 15TH 1920

Catherine Street runs north-west from the Aldwych to Russell Street. It is eminent not only for its two theatres, the Duchess and Drury Lane, but also for two taverns which are worth a visit for the reason that both contain a collection of old theatre-programmes and playbills. One is the Opera Tavern and the other the Sir John Falstaff, which had for its inn-sign, till very recently, a painting of the modern actor who gave us the best Falstaff in the last fifty years, that of Sir Ralph Richardson. It was in one of these two taverns that, as legend says, Richard Brinsley Sheridan (Pl. 17) sat while his theatre—the Theatre Royal, Drury Lane—was burning itself to the ground. He had been summoned from the Houses of Parliament to see the conflagration. Instead of helping to save anything he went into this tavern and ordered a bottle of wine and a glass. Someone finding him there asked him why he did not join the rescue squad, and received the answer: 'Cannot a man enjoy a glass of wine by his own fireside?' It may be almost the most hackneyed, but it is certainly one of the choicest of old theatrical stories.

The Duchess Theatre was not built until 1929, and it is for me particularly associated with the best of the early plays of J. B. Priestley —*Eden End* (1934), *Cornelius* (1935), *Time and the Conways* (1937). No better plays were written for the English stage between the two wars, and Ralph Richardson again distinguished himself in the first two of them. *Eden End*, a semi-tragedy set in the Yorkshire dales and concerning a doctor and his two daughters, one of whom became an actress, was a favourite play of mine from the start. One reason, which has nothing to do with dramatic criticism, was that the doctor was played by a sterling old actor, James Harcourt, who was in both looks and behaviour remarkably like my dear father, who was a man of Westmorland. The dialogue throughout was Priestley, that man of Yorkshire, at his best, and I can still in the mind's ear hear this doctor, coming in late at night from a case of childbirth and saying to his two daughters, the stay-at-home one and the one with the reputation as an actress: 'Mrs. Sugden's been delivered of a man-child so big and so like William Sugden that I felt like offering it a pipe of tobacco. Ah, well—I'm tired!'

At the other end of Catherine Street is the great Theatre Royal, Drury Lane, whose splendid façade is in the street proper, whose colonnaded side takes up the whole length of Russell Street from Catherine Street to Drury Lane, and whose rear is in Drury Lane proper. It is the oldest theatre in the land, the first house of the name, more than seventy years older than Covent Garden Theatre, which became the Opera House, and more than fifty years older than the Haymarket Theatre, which was built in 1720. It is a curious fact that the first theatre of the name opened in Brydges Street in 1663, with a comedy by Beaumont and Fletcher, *The Humorous Lieutenant*; while the second opened, in Drury Lane itself in 1674, with another comedy by Beaumont and Fletcher, *The Beggar's Bush*. The third, which was Sheridan's theatre and which perished as we have seen, opened in 1794 with a concert of sacred music. The entirely rebuilt Drury Lane, No 4, was opened in 1812 with a performance of *Hamlet*. This was preceded by an address written by Lord Byron and delivered by R. W. Elliston, who was soon to become an actor-manager at the new theatre.

The façade and the colonnade of the great theatre are as they have been for well over a century. But the interior has been entirely reconstructed —without interfering, it would seem, with the walks of the traditional ghost, that of an eighteenth-century gallant who was slain in a duel and hidden behind a wall. My own particular fancy is that the ghost is that of Edmund Kean's Shylock or Richard. It was in the old Drury Lane Theatre that Kean (Pl. 34) had his initial triumph in the former character on a cold January night in the year 1814, when he had the marvellous luck to have William Hazlitt in his sparse but responsive audience.

It is a theatre building immensely rich in recollections. It is in its atmosphere totally different from that of the Opera House, so near and yet so far, and not in sight of one another. They are like two great hostesses who happen to be at the same party, but who avoid each other because their gowns are rather similar.

The four statues in the rotunda at the back of the foyer are Shakespeare, David Garrick, Edmund Kean and—rather disconcertingly—Michael William Balfe, who wrote widely popular early Victorian ballad-operas. More than once I have overheard first-nighters at Drury Lane say in passing: 'Why not Ivor Novello instead of this mysterious Balfe?' Why not (one supposes), since Novello kept the theatre open and packed for twenty years with his own widely popular brand of sentimental ballad-operas?

My own pleasantest memories of Drury Lane Theatre have been not of events in the auditorium, but of the annual meetings of the Ellen Terry Fellowship in the board-room upstairs. There, year after year, in daffodil time—and with the room liberally adorned with daffodils—gracious old players celebrated the birthday with Shakespeare and with reminiscences. It is a Fellowship which has, sadly, been disbanded.

At the left-hand corner of the great theatre's façade is a less-than-life-size bust of its supreme impresario, Sir Augustus Harris (1851–96). This effigy has no inscription whatever except the name 'Augustus Harris' and the words 'Erected by Public Subscription'. The bust is framed by two little bronze pillars encrusted with musical instruments, and it surmounts a very dry-looking drinking fountain over which, on either side, bend two debauched-looking cherubs. Someone wittily nicknamed Sir Augustus 'Druriolanus', and the nickname has lasted better than the name. Yet with all his faults of grandiosity and lavishness, he had the theatre in his blood. His grandfather, Joseph Glossop, built the transpontine Coburg Theatre which became the Victoria, and later still the Old Vic. His father, Augustus Glossop Harris

1. Inigo Jones, who laid out the Piazza—'the secular heart of Covent Garden'—and designed St Paul's church in 1631. 2. I pause on my way along the colonnade of the charter market which has occupied the square since 1830.

3. 'A perspective view' of 1751.

4. Sandby's view, through the arcades on the north, of the east side before it was destroyed by fire in 1769.

5. The New Charter Market, 1830, consisted of three parallel buildings with outer colonnades and a central avenue. James Butler's sign on the building on the south-west corner was still to be seen in 1972.

6. Richard Wilson, Peter Pindar's 'honest Wilson', a talent neglected in his lifetime, lived for several years in the Great Piazza. 7. A resident of the Little Piazza was Mrs Mary Robinson—called Perdita after her best known Shakespearean part—who queened it at Drury Lane from 1776 to 1780. 8. Sir William Davenant, poet laureate, politician and dramatist, was granted by Charles II in 1663 the patent under which the Opera House still functions.

9. Thomas Rowlandson satirized the folly and vanity of the rich as well as of the poor. 'Box Lobby Loungers', 1786, is an Opera House scene with rakes, beaux, courtesans and (left) a bawd with play-bills and fruit.

10. Edmund Waller, Cavalier poet and politician, an occasional resident in Bow Street.

11. 'Pretty, witty' Nell Gwynne, born near Drury Lane in 1650, grew up to bewitch her King.

12. John Kemble, leading tragedian at Drury Lane for many years and later manager.

13. No. 21 Russell Street, formerly Will's Coffee House, where Dryden reigned until 1701.

15. James Boswell lived in this house in Great Queen Street, lamentably pulled down in 1913.

16. Sir Richard Steele, early dramatic critic and essayist, was the original *Tatler*. The Lion's Head letterbox at Buttons (14), accepted contributions.

17. R. B. Sheridan, Irish-born wit, author of at least two immortal comedies, and manager of The Theatre Royal, Drury Lane.

18. James Boswell often visited the market by day as well as by night, but preferably without Dr Johnson.

19–23.
Within living memory the Lyceum was the theatre of Henry Irving (inset) and Ellen Terry. On 23rd May 1938, the Henry Irving Centenary matinee was held in the rebuilt theatre (a latecomer, I was photographed standing in the side aisle). Above right: Irving superbly autocratic as Digby Grant in *Two Roses* by James Albery. Ellen Terry (left) as Juliet with Mrs Stirling as the Nurse, in 1882; right, as Imogen in *Cymbeline*, 1894.

24. Distinguished apparition, drawn by Francis Marshall to my directions. She was Baroness Burdett-Coutts.

25. A magazine cover endeared to generations of readers.

26. Versatile manager of the old Gaiety, John Hollingshead.

27. Pert, nimble spirit of mirth, Nelly Farren of the old Gaiety burlesques.

28. William Hazlitt, self-portrait. Unsurpassed Sultan of dramatic critics.

29. Running towards the Coliseum (left) and the Duke of York's Theatre (right), St Martin's Lane is illusively blocked by the great portico of St Martin-in-the-Fields. 30. James Gibbs, Scottish architect of St Martin-in-the-Fields, from the bust in the church.

31. William Terriss, ideal hero of Adelphi melodrama. He was murdered in 1897. 32. London welcomed the 'sublime Italian actress' Eleonora Duse, memorable at the Strand (then Waldorf) Theatre.

33. David Garrick, shining as always, but in a dim tragedy by James Thomson, *Tancred and Sigismunda*.

34. The painter George Clint, Covent Garden born, catches the evil power of Massinger's Sir Giles Overreach, sensationally portrayed by Edmund Kean. The painting was presented to the Garrick Club by Sir Henry Irving in 1889.

35. The Nag's Head, Floral Street, fronted by the author, exhibits a fine collection of theatrical prints.

36, 37. At my King Street front door, once that of actor G. F. Cooke; and my char Liddy Shipp, plucky, cheerful, intensely Cockney.

38. 'The house of Lord Archer in Covent
Garden', *c.* 1754, is still in the market. The
building later became Evans's Grand Hotel
and Supper Rooms and then the headquarters
of the National Sporting Club.   39. Nos. 29–30
Bedford Street in 1901. This was the publisher's
first West End office. The gateway is the entrance to Inigo Place and the churchyard of
St Paul's, Covent Garden.

40. St Paul's, 'the actors' church', must remain the sacred heart of my Covent Garden.

(1825–73), became manager of the Princess's Theatre after the reign of Charles Kean, and was later manager of Covent Garden Opera House for twenty-seven years. Harris himself—Sir Augustus Henry Glossop Harris—managed Covent Garden and Drury Lane in turn for almost as long; was part-author of several very successful Drury Lane melodramas with titles such as *Cheer, Boys, Cheer!*; brought the Christmas pantomime to a state of unprecedented splendour; and made possible the visits from abroad of Mme Ristori, the Comédie Française and the Meiningen Players from Germany.

Bernard Shaw, first as music critic at the Opera, and later as dramatic critic at the Lane, attacked Sir Augustus consistently and wittily—even when he died at the early age of forty-four of his own superhuman industry. Just as Shaw never forgave Irving for not being Ibsen-minded, so he never forgave Harris for not being Wagner-minded. Harris had somewhere in Shaw's hearing called Wagner's *Rheingold* a 'damned pantomime'; and Shaw, the Perfect Wagnerite, never forgot it. Personally I would much rather see a good English pantomime—especially one at the Lane in the days of Druriolanus!— than any Wagner whatsoever in any language. But it is much more to the point if I say that I once saw Sir Augustus Harris's daughter. She was an actress with something like her father's grit and industry. This was in Glasgow in 1924 in my student days. She was my first Cleopatra, and had already played almost every other female part in Shakespeare. She was stately, if not overwhelming. Her name was Florence Glossop Harris, and she was Henry Baynton's leading lady.

In nearby Russell Street stood Button's Coffee House. It was established in 1712 or 1713 and existed till the middle of the century. Its founder, Daniel Button, had formerly been a servant of the Countess of Warwick whom Addison was to marry in 1716. It was Addison himself who set up Button as Master of the Coffee House, 'and thither Addison transferred the company from Tom's Coffee House'.

The house was celebrated for its Lion's Head letterbox (Pl. 14). In his *Guardian*, issue No. 114 dated 22nd July 1713, Richard Steele wrote as follows: 'I think myself obliged to acquaint the public, that the Lion's Head, of which I advertised them about a fortnight ago, is now erected at Button's Coffee-house, in Russell Street, Covent Garden, where it opens its mouth at all hours for the reception of such intelligence as shall be thrown into it. . . . It is planted on the western side of the Coffee-house, holding its paws under the chin upon a box, which contains everything he swallows.' There are frequent mentions of this early and most famous Coffee-house in the *Guardian,* and in Steele's *Lover* (for 6th March 1714) it is coupled with a reference—apparently the only one in existence—to Shanley's, obviously another and more accessible Covent Garden resort. The passage gives a clear and charming indication that the coffee-house had rapidly become 'the thing' and the place to visit: 'The two theatres, and all the public Coffee-houses, I shall constantly frequent, but principally the Coffee-house under my lodge, Button's, and the play-house in Covent Garden; but as I set up for the judge of pleasures, I think it necessary to assign particular places of resort to my young gentlemen as they come to town, who cannot expect to pop in at Button's on the first day of their arrival in town. I recommend it, therefore, to young men to frequent Shanley's some days before they take upon them to appear at Button's. . . .'

In the days of Addison and Steele, Button's was regarded as the centre of literature and was greatly frequented by the wits and celebrities of the time. But its company clearly lost much of its character after Steele's retirement to Wales and Addison's death in 1719.

In the *Daily Advertiser* for 5th October 1731 appeared this melancholy news-item. 'On Sunday morning died, after three days' illness, Mr. Button, who formerly kept Button's Coffee-house—a very noted house for wits, being the place where the Lyon produced the famous Tatlers and Spectators, written by the late Mr. Secretary Addison and Sir Richard Steele, Knt., which works will transmit their names with honour to posterity.' It is on record that in its last days Button's was frequently visited by James Maclaine, the 'fashionable highwayman' of Irish birth and Scottish blood, who used to pay 'particular attention to the barmaid of the Coffee-house, the daughter of the landlord'. Maclaine was executed at Tyburn on 3rd October 1750, when he was only twenty-six. The previous year he had the honour of robbing and slightly wounding Horace Walpole when that witty gossip was returning from Holland House through Hyde Park. He also robbed Lord Eglinton on Hounslow Heath. The *Dictionary of National Biography* has a racy account of his brilliantly bad life. Walpole himself tells us that on the first Sunday after his condemnation three thousand people went to see Maclaine in Newgate, and White's Club, it was stated, visited him *en masse.* We are told also that many portraits of 'the gentleman highwayman' or 'the ladies hero', as he was called, are still in existence, and the account concludes with a somewhat equivocal description of the rascal's physique: 'His features were good, but his face broad and pitted with smallpox. He was of sandy complexion, square-shouldered, and well made downwards.'

When Button's came to an end the Lion's Head letterbox changed hands. It was first removed to the Shakespeare Tavern 'under the Piazza', and thereafter it seems to have been purchased by various other taverns in Covent Garden Market which tended automatically to change their names to The Lion's Head. In 1804 it was sold to Mr Richardson, the proprietor of Richardson's Hotel (as No. 43 King Street was then called). Mr Richardson paid £17 10s. for it. From him it was eventually bought, for an unspecified sum, by the Duke of Bedford to be placed among the treasures of art and antiquity in Woburn Abbey, where it is to be seen to this day.

It may be called the earliest of pillar-boxes. The lion was modelled on the antique Egyptian lion, and was designed by William Hogarth. It was inscribed as follows:

> CERVANTUR MAGNIS ISTI CERVICIBUS UNGUES
> NON NISI DELICTA PASCITUR ILLE FERA

About this inscription it may be observed that, though both the lines are from Martial, they are not consecutive, but come from two separate epigrams, 23 and 61 in Book I. These epigrams are both on the same subject, and refer to the curious practice of training a lion to allow a hare to run in and out of its jaws unharmed.

There is, furthermore, a misprint in each line quoted. In the first line *Cervantur* should be *Servantur*, and in the second *delicta* should be *delecta*. The point and meaning of the couplet, doubtless, is that Sir Richard Steele's paper, the *Guardian*, proposes to be a guardian of the lowly and innocent, and intends to strike only at the 'necks of the mighty'.

And now for one of the major meetings in literary history! It was in Thomas Davies's book shop in Russell Street that Boswell first made the acquaintance of Dr Johnson. Boswell's own account is incomparable:

'This [1763] is to me a memorable year; for in it I had the happiness to obtain the acquaintance of that extraordinary man, whose memoirs I am now writing; an acquaintance which I shall ever esteem as one of the most fortunate circumstances of my life. Though then but two-and-twenty, I had for several years read his works with delight and instruction, and had the highest reverence for their author, which had grown up in my fancy into a kind of mysterious veneration. . . . Mr. Thomas Davies, the actor, who then kept a bookseller's shop in Russel-street, Covent-garden, told me that Johnson was very much his friend, and came frequently to his house, where he more than once invited me to meet him: where by some unlucky accident or other he was prevented from coming to us. . . . Mr. Davies recollected many of Johnson's remarkable sayings, and was one of the best of the many imitators of his voice and manner, while relating them. . . . He increased my impatience more and more to see the extraordinary man whose works I highly valued, and whose conversation was reported to be so peculiarly excellent.

'At last, on Monday the 16th of May, when I was sitting in Mr. Davies's back-parlour, after having drunk tea with him and Mrs. Davies, Johnson unexpectedly came into the shop, and Mr. Davies having perceived him through the glass-door in the room in which we were sitting, advancing towards us,—he announced his awful approach to me, somewhat in the manner of an actor in the part of Horatio, when he addresses Hamlet on the appearance of his father's ghost, "Look, my Lord, it comes." I found that I had a very perfect idea of Johnson's figure, from the portrait of him painted by Sir Joshua Reynolds soon after he had published his Dictionary, in the attitude of sitting in his easy chair in deep meditation. . . . Mr. Davies mentioned my name, and respectfully introduced me to him. I was much agitated; and recollecting his prejudice against the Scotch, of which I had heard much, I said to Davies: "Don't tell where I come from."—"From Scotland," cried Davies, roguishly. "Mr. Johnson, (said I) I do indeed come from Scotland, but I cannot help it." I am willing to flatter myself that I meant this as light pleasantry to soothe and conciliate him, and not as an humiliating abasement at the expence of my country. But however that may be, this speech was somewhat unlucky; for with that quickness of wit for which he was so remarkable, he seized the expression, "come from Scotland," which I used in the sense of being of that country; and, as if I had said that I had come away from it, or left it, retorted, "That, Sir, I find is what a very great many of your countrymen cannot help." This stroke stunned me a good deal; and when we had sat down, I felt myself not a little embarrassed, and apprehensive of what might come next. He then addressed himself to Davies: "What do you think of Garrick? He has refused me an order for the play for Miss Williams, because he knows the house will be full, and that an order would be worth three shillings." Eager to take any opening to get into conversation with him, I ventured to say, "O, Sir, I cannot think Mr. Garrick would grudge such a trifle to you." "Sir (said he, with a stern look) I have known David Garrick longer than you have done; and I know no right you have to talk to me on the subject." Perhaps I deserved this check; for it was rather presumptuous in me, an entire stranger to express any doubt on the justice of his animadversion upon his old acquaintance and pupil. I now felt myself much mortified, and began to think, that the hope which I had long indulged of obtaining his acquaintance was blasted. And, in truth, had not my ardour been uncommonly strong, and my resolution been uncommonly persevering, so rough a reception might have deterred me for ever from making any further attempts. Fortunately, however, I remained upon the field not wholly discomfited; and was soon rewarded by hearing some of his conversation. . . .'

[There follow some eight or nine examples of Johnson's wise wit and witty wisdom, and then the account of the very first of the encounters of this exquisitely complementary pair concludes characteristically] . . .

'I was highly pleased with the extraordinary vigour of his conversation, and regretted that I was drawn away from it by an engagement at another place. I had, for a part of the evening, been left alone with him, and had ventured to make an observation now and then, which he received very civilly; so I was satisfied that though there was a roughness in his manner, there was no ill-nature in his disposition. Davies followed me to the door, and when I complained to him a little of the hard blows which the great man had given me, he kindly took it upon him to console me by saying, "Don't be uneasy. I can see he likes you very well."'

I know of no better account of a first meeting. Boswell tells us that he wrote his account on the same day—and it seems to me that it would be heinous and ill-advised to truncate, transcribe, cut or alter his actual description. The momentous meeting happened in Russell Street, which runs from the Piazza to Drury Lane and crosses Bow Street on its way.

At the corner of Russell Street and Bow Street there stood (easily within our own time) the offices of *The Era*, one of London's two major theatrical newspapers under the editorship of George Bishop, the journalist. This was a *vrai bonhomme* who had the theatre in his bones though he had the austere features of a born ecclesiastic. He tells us in his autobiography that he could never summon up much interest in the cinema, and when he resigned from the editorship of *The Era* in 1931 it was because the paper had been acquired by a film company. The new proprietors attempted to turn the fine old journal (with a record of a hundred years of devotion to things theatrical) into a trade paper in which the films came first and the theatre second. *The Era* did not long survive George Bishop's departure. Its only serious rival (again for scores of years) still survives it. This is *The Stage*, which looks like lasting as long as the theatre itself. As is fitting, its offices are likewise in Covent Garden, in the eastern end of Tavistock Street just round the corner.

Also in Russell Street is another theatre, the Fortune, with a Scottish Presbyterian church, known as Crown Court Church, alongside it. The Fortune looks small enough to be packable inside the great shell of Drury Lane Theatre itself, and would probably occupy no more space than the latter's stage does. It was built in 1924, the first new theatre in London after the First World War. Its site had been that of the Albion Tavern, a favourite haunt of actors for a hundred years previously. I have just said that Crown Court Church was 'alongside' the Fortune Theatre; it would be more correct to say that the two buildings are 'intertwined'. The Fortune was meant originally to be called the Crown because of the adjacent paved alley which is Crown Court. The entrance to the church in Russell Street has the theatre built over it and under it. This is, architecturally, a curious and remarkable piece of construction. The passage-way traverses the theatre's entire length, stage included, on one of its sides, yet is not discernible from within. The result is a complete and rare example of the union of The Stage and The Church. It would be agreeable to discover that this double site, where formerly, as I have said, stood the Albion Tavern, had also been the site of Davies's book shop where Boswell first met Dr Johnson. But, less happily, the site of Davies's

book shop is now taken up by a prosaic Telephone Exchange building
Or was!

And so we come at last to Bow Street itself, which has to begin with
—and directly facing one another—Covent Garden Opera House
(already dealt with) and perhaps the best-known Police Station and
Magistrate's Court in the entire world. On its site there originally
stood a mansion belonging to the Duke of Bedford, which became the
home of the Fieldings. Both the blind Sir John Fielding and his more
famous brother, Henry the novelist, were practising magistrates here.
The Court part of this building was destroyed by the Gordon Rioters
in 1780. In a house on the same site once lived the Cavalier poet,
Edmund Waller (Pl. 10), who has immortalized himself in a single
lyric, 'Go, Lovely Rose'. Bow Street Police Station has been rebuilt at
least four times, and has sometimes—to the frank confusion of the
chroniclers—been re-erected on the opposite side of the street, either
just north or just south of the Opera House.

In the Cock Tavern, near-by and long-vanished, actors and dramatists forgathered as they did at the Albion. On its roof in the year
1663 there took place a notorious orgy, described and deplored by
Pepys, when three young rips—Sir Charles Sedley (a dramatist himself), Lord Buckhurst and Sir Thomas Ogle—got hopelessly 'high',
stripped on the roof and scandalized even the most unprincipled
marketeers, 'going through performances not usually associated with
publicity'. When a crowd gathered beneath the tavern it was harangued
by Sedley in terms both obscene and blasphemous. The roysterers were
eventually arrested and carried off to prison. They were brought
before Lord Chief Justice Foster, and Pepys tells what happened: 'My
Lord and the rest of the judges did all of them round give him [Sedley]
a most high reproofe; my Lord Chief Justice saying that it was for
him, and such wicked wretches as he was, that God's anger and
judgments hung over us, calling him Sirrah! many times. It seems
they have bound him to his good behaviour, there being no law
against him for it, in £5,000.' All three of these ignoble nobles were
heavily fined and tried to intercede with the King himself. But in
vain! They appear to have exposed themselves in every possible sense
of the term.

This same Cock Tavern was a regular resort of William Wycherley,
who lived opposite. He had unwisely married the very jealous Countess

of Drogheda, and this most virile of Restoration dramatists—nick-named Manly Wycherley—was espied there by his lady from her windows opposite. In the words of the old chronicler John Dennis: 'If he were at any time with his friends, he was obliged to leave the windows open, that the lady might see there were no women in his company, or she would be immediately in a downright raving condition.'

In old memoirs we catch an unusual glimpse—a whole century ahead—of Henry Irving in his early days playing many parts, mainly villainous, in Alfred Wigan's fine company at the Queen's Theatre in Long Acre. He was beginning to realize that he was happiest in the company of fellow-actors whose humour and sympathies came near to his own, with their arduous rehearsals by day—with the nightly repetition of an agreeable and rewarding part—and with, between them, the lavish yet miraculously cheap banquets of roast meat which he, J. L. Toole and Lionel Brough would consume standing side by side at the counter of the ham-and-beef shop at the corner of Russell Street and Bow Street. Those weeks at the Queen's Theatre were the happiest he had ever known. Little could Irving know while he ate his supper that at that point he was only a very few minutes' walk away from the Lyceum where, in 1871, he was to become leading man under Colonel Bateman's management, and where in 1878 he was to be joined by Ellen Terry to become the greatest actor of his day and to reign until the very end of the century.

Where Bow Street is intersected by Russell Street, and at the north corner, stood another old tavern—another century back—which eventually became Will's Coffee-House (Pl. 13), so called after its landlord William Unwin. Here John Dryden held court every day, winter and summer. Jonathan Swift, too, became a regular frequenter of Will's. He has many references to Covent Garden as a haunt of wits. In his preface to *The Tale of a Tub* he writes: 'You may preach in Covent Garden against Foppery and Fornication, and *something else*' [his own italics, whatever they may signify!]. And in the same curious book he has an allegory of three sons, born at one birth, who took the town when they reached a proper age. In the following quotation I have modernized Swift's spelling but kept his picturesque use of capitals: 'They Writ, and Rallied, and Rhymed, and Sung, and Said, and said Nothing. They Drank, and Fought, and Whored, and Slept, and Swore, and took Snuff. They went to new Plays on the first Night, haunted the Chocolate Houses, beat the Watch, lay on Bulks [stalls in front of shops], and got Claps. They bilked Hackney Coachmen, ran in Debt with Shopkeepers, and lay with their Wives. They killed Bailiffs, kicked Fiddlers down Stairs, ate at Locket [a fashionable ordinary at Charing Cross], loitered at Will's.' With this teeming vision of Jonathan Swift we may take our leave of Bow Street.

But let us, before leaving it, notice Martlett Court, which is easily overlooked. Today it is a dull and featureless passage opposite the Royal Opera and the rather battered conservatory which is used as a storehouse by the Foreign Fruit Market. Martlett Court has on its left nothing but the side of Bow Street Police Station, and on its right nothing but a brand-new telephone exchange building. But two hundred years ago even little Martlett Court teemed with theatrical life. Ned Shuter was living at No. 2 when he advertised his own benefit; Shuter (whom we shall see later in his cups) was once declared by David Garrick himself to be a comic genius of an actor. In this same little street G. F. Cooke lived when he first came to London, and Charles Dibdin in his memoirs tells of the hard task he had in carrying the brandy-soaked tragedian back to his lodging here. Here, too, lived John O'Keefe, the Dublin-born playwright whose excellent farce *Wild Oats* deserves revival because its chief character, Rover, was a favourite of many of the old actors, Rover, himself, being a professional actor soaked in Shakespeare. Last and by no means least, there lived here the humbly born actress Harriot Mellon, who married first Thomas Coutts, the banker, and then the ninth Duke of St Albans. She enters this book again elsewhere. Let me only say here that it was in her lodging in Martlett Court that she used to cook choice little dinners for her famous banker before she married him. He was then eighty years old, but the marriage was exceedingly happy till death came between and left her an exceedingly wealthy widow.

Incidentally this actress came to London from the provinces on the recommendation of Garrick, who happened to see her playing Rosalind at Stafford. An old *Thespian Dictionary* in my possession reveals that 'at Stafford Miss Mellon was favoured with the friendship of Mr. Wright, the banker, with whose sister and daughters she lived in habits of intimacy'. Harriot would seem, in short, to have had a pretty predilection for bankers throughout most of her career (or at least until she became a Duchess at the end of it).

CHAPTER FIVE

NEWS ACROSS THE STRAND

At the very beginning of our third segment of the Covent Garden district—it is bounded on the south side by The Strand from Wellington Street to Trafalgar Square—we arrive at another old and distinguished theatre which is now in an undistinguished condition—to wit, a dance-hall. This is the Lyceum, which still within living memory was the Lyceum of Henry Irving and Ellen Terry (Pls. 19–23). The first building on this site and with this name was opened in 1772 as a 'Room for Exhibitions, Concerts and Entertainments'. Its façade was in The Strand and not, as now, in Wellington Street. In 1809 this building was licensed as a theatre for the summer months only, and was known as The Theatre Royal English Opera. In 1830 the building was destroyed by fire, but in 1834 it had been rebuilt as The Royal Lyceum and English Opera House, and its quite imposing and dignified façade faced Wellington Street as it does today. This theatre remained till 1903, the end of the Irving-Terry régime. In 1904 it was entirely rebuilt except for the back wall (in Burleigh Street) and the frontage (in Wellington Street), and it was reopened as a music-hall and called simply The Lyceum. In 1907 the music-hall became a house of popular robust melodrama, and at its opening a writer in *The Graphic* made the observation:

'Many may regret that the mighty have fallen, but there is no doubt that the new managers of the Lyceum have done a wise thing in re-introducing substantial and sound melodrama to the West End of London. And melodrama is, at any rate, several steps higher than the two-shows-a-night music-hall to which the famous old theatre descended a little time ago. In visiting *Her Love Against the World* you leave your critical faculties at home. There is no use for them at the new Lyceum.'

The theatre closed for good with some performances of *Hamlet* (John Gielgud and Fay Compton). This was in July 1939, last year of the peace between the two world wars. It was reopened as a dance-hall in October 1945, and bathetically as such it has remained to this day.

The historian of this theatre—the late A. E. Wilson, completing the work of the late Arthur Beales after the latter's death at the age of forty-six—divides its existence into three well-defined parts: the pre-Irving period (1771–1871), the long Irving régime (1871–1901) and the post-Irving period (1904–39). Before the theatre in any form or under any title existed this was the site of Burleigh or Cecil House, built by Sir William Cecil, Lord Treasurer to Queen Elizabeth I. An old account describes the now vanished mansion as 'a noble pile, built with brick, and adorned with four square turrets'. It faced The Strand and its gardens extended from the west side of the Garden Walk of Wimbledon House (near the present site of Wellington Street) to the Green Lane westward (which is now called Southampton Street). This mansion was later renamed Exeter House, and after the Great Fire of London it was occupied by members of the Doctors' Commons; and the Courts of the Arches and of the Admiralty were carried on there.

For the first century of its existence the Lyceum Theatre housed every kind of exhibition and entertainment—wild-animal shows and menageries, wax-works, musical evenings under the great Charles Dibdin, tight-rope dancing and tumbling. When Drury Lane Theatre was burned down in 1809 its company chose the Lyceum as a temporary home, a licence having been obtained from the Lord Chamberlain. Samuel Beazley, architect of the new theatre, had also designed the Adelphi and the Strand theatres. He moreover designed the colonnade of the new theatre in Catherine Street, the Theatre Royal, Drury Lane, as it remains to this day. Fanny Kelly opened the new Lyceum with a prologue. In childhood she had played Prince Arthur to the Constance of Mrs Siddons.

The Lyceum was the first London theatre to use gas lighting for its stage, in August 1817, though the Olympia had used it in the auditorium as early as 1815. The theatre's history throughout the nineteenth century was extremely varied and complicated. In 1818 the elder Charles Mathews gave his popular solo performance called 'Mathews at Home'. He was engaged there for seven years at an

annual salary of £1,000. The tragedian G. F. Cooke (much admired
by the great Edmund Kean) appeared there as Frankenstein's monster
in 1823, and in the following year Kean himself acted there. In 1830
the house was burned down. It was rebuilt and reopened in 1834. The
main entrance was now in Wellington Street. Here in 1835 came
Frédérick Lemaître from Paris, an actor said in all ways to resemble
the English Kean.

In 1842 it was renamed the American Amphitheatre and housed a
wild-beast show. In 1844 it went over to legitimate drama, the patent
rights of the two great theatres, Covent Garden and Drury Lane,
having been finally broken by the Licensing Act of the previous year.
The Keeleys took it over and made a success with several dramatizations of the day's most popular novelist, Charles Dickens. These lasted
till 1847 when the famous Mme Vestris (Mrs Charles Mathews) took
over. In 1863 came another fashionable Shakespearean actor, Charles
Fechter, who had played in French and English in Europe and
America, with equal success. He was the first actor to play Armand
Duval in *La Dame aux Camélias* (1852). His revolutionary performance
of Hamlet in English first won him fame in London; he was praised
for abandoning old traditions in the part. But the great critic G. H.
Lewes said that while his Hamlet was one of the best he had ever
seen, his Othello was one of the worst.

When I first came to London the Lyceum was still a home of melodrama under the management of the Melville Brothers, Walter and
Frederick, who kept it such for thirty years and came of an intensely
theatrical family. These two remarkable and prosperous brothers—
actors as well as managers in their time—ran the Lyceum from May
1910 until July 1939. They were an odd and unconventional pair who
shunned publicity. They would not hear of rehearsing on a Sunday,
however behind-hand the rehearsals might be. They liked employing
the same actors year after year. They liked writing their own plays. I
saw only one of these during the Melville régime. But I know that now
I never shall be certain whether it was *The Girl who took the Wrong
Turning* or *The Worst Woman in London* (both of which were the work
of Frederick). Or it may possibly have been *The Bad Girl of the Family*,
which was the work of Walter. The titles, anyhow, are generic and
typical. The Lyceum melodrama was rank, full-blooded, strong, meaty,
not very literary or even literate, but always ineffably and intensely
enjoyable. The Melville brothers did not care much about the Press

and did not go out of their way to invite the more responsible critics. But they had their huge reliable public very much as Christmas pantomimes still have. And, incidentally, the Christmas pantomime at the Lyceum itself always ran right into the spring like the best pantomimes in the provinces. They had a public prosperity which was immune from the barbs of puny criticism. Our supreme authority on melodrama, Willson Disher, justly sums up the achievement of the Melville brothers: 'Not until they had acted melodrama, stage-managed melodrama, produced melodrama, and made melodrama pay did they then *write* melodrama. They began by re-writing melodrama under conditions that resembled authorship on the Elizabethan stage. Loads of manuscripts appeared to have no copyright because each represented such a succession of literary thefts that the original authors had been forgotten.'

Bert Hammond, who was for many years the Melvilles' house-manager at the Lyceum, has given us a lively picture of what went on there every Christmas:

'At the Lyceum we always believed in slavishly following the fairy story and giving simple fun and a lot for the money. We tried to entertain both grown-ups and the children. For our first performance on Christmas Eve, which we called a *répétition générale*, we invited many poor children from different districts of London, usually about 2,500. Sometimes these performances went on from two in the afternoon until well after six at night, but still the children stayed and wanted more. These youngsters greeted everyone and everything, including any mistakes, with uproarious applause, and according to their teachers this show lasted them the whole of the year.

'After this performance the actors, comedians and company would be called together to arrange for cutting the show down to the respectable length of about three hours. This caused great disappointment to the comics, who never seemed to tire of their own antics and were just as happy as the kids. But a four-and-a-half-hour show couldn't be done, and the Melville brothers had to be very firm.

'Another great occasion in the Lyceum pantomime season was the visit by the Greenwich Royal Hospital School boys, the coming sailors of the Royal and Merchant navies, well over 2,000 of them, who used to march up The Strand with their band playing at the head of the column and their diminutive drum-major marching in front. This caused a great sensation, to say nothing of the dislocation of the traffic.'

I recall—and was very much present at—one of the Lyceum's very last productions. This was a special matinee on 23rd May 1938, organized by the *Daily Telegraph* in honour of the centenary of the birth of Henry Irving (Pl. 20). The programme consisted of excerpts from plays in which the great actor had appeared at the Lyceum. Thus Laurence Olivier appeared as Jingle, Godfrey Tearle was Mathias in *The Bells*, Owen Nares was Charles I, Wilfrid Lawson played a scene from *The Corsican Brothers*, Robert Farquharson was Louis XI, and Ralph Richardson was Becket. My boss at the time, James Agate, treated this charity occasion uncharitably: 'The matinee was in honour of the greatest actor any of us has seen or is likely to see. It was finely inspired, beautifully pageantried, and executed by the players, many of them with a cheerful resignation beyond all praise. One by one they went to annihilation as determinedly as Charles I went to the scaffold. "Remember Irving!" each seemed to be saying, with a look in the tail of his eye which signified: "And for heaven's sake forget about us! This is not our job and we know it."'

Between these excerpts we saw interludes or tableaux including a reproduction of a Lyceum pit queue in 1880, a supper party in the theatre's famous Beefsteak Room, and an imagined visit, to Irving's dressing-room, by the Baroness Burdett-Coutts (of whom more at the end of this chapter). The baroness was portrayed by Dame Lilian Braithwaite. But for me personally this matinee was most of all made memorable by the fact that the *Daily Telegraph*, photographing the auditorium just after the arrival of Queen Mary, made me *almost* as conspicuous a figure standing under the box adjoining Her Majesty's. I had arrived late and had been unable to get into my seat in the stalls in time.

The great theatre, which was bought for destruction by the London County Council, has never been destroyed. It remains a dance-hall. *The Stage* asked at the time of its purchase: 'Would Irving during his régime have let the Lyceum to be used as a dance-hall?' And answered its own question: 'He would rather have died.'

The Strand itself is one of the oldest streets in London and there is mention of its existence under that name as early as the year 1245. In Plantagenet times it genuinely was a strand, sloping down to the River Thames with only an occasional house here and there. Till the middle of the fourteenth century The Strand was an open highway with on the south side a few large mansion houses whose gardens extended down to the river. The traffic consisted mainly of foot-passengers and horse-riders, carriages being almost unknown until the time of Queen Elizabeth. In those early times—pre-Covent-Garden times—The Strand was the connecting link between the City of London, the village of Charing and the City of Westminster. The south side of The Strand is none of my business here, but I cannot forbear to mention that its major buildings in those early days were mansion houses: the Palace of the Savoy, extending from Wellington Street to Savoy Street; Worcester House, later called Beaufort House, on the site of Savoy Court; Salisbury House, built by the son of the great Lord Burleigh, which stood on the site of the Hotel Cecil, now replaced by the gigantic Shell Building; Durham House, extending back from Durham House Place to Adam Street. York House, residence of Buckingham (formerly that of the Bishops of Norwich and then of the Archbishops of York) occupied the site of the present Buckingham Street and some of its neighbours. The mansion of the Hungerfords, burnt down in 1669, occupied the land where now stands Charing Cross railway station and hotel. Northumberland House stood roughly where Northumberland Avenue now stands.

The north side of The Strand also had its great mansion houses in the far-away past, but they were distinctly fewer in number. When the great mansions were destroyed—most of them towards the end of the seventeenth century—the streets and buildings which replaced them were generally named after the old owners of the property. Thus at the east end of The Strand we had Norfolk Street until very recently and we still have Somerset House; towards the west end we still have the Savoy Hotel and the Savoy Theatre, with numerous streets and lanes all with the word Savoy in their title. On the site of the Durham House stables—now numbered 52–64 on the south side—was built the New Exchange or Britain's Bourse early in the reign of James I. This was a two-storey market and bazaar, often mentioned in Restoration comedies. At No. 59 was located from 1737 till 1904 the first Coutts's Bank. This had been established in St Martin's Lane in 1692 as

'Middleton and Campbell' and opened in The Strand, in 1737, under that name. Later it was 'Campbell and Bruce'; then, in 1754, one James Coutts became a partner, and the style of the banking firm was changed to 'Campbell and Coutts'. Thomas Coutts, grandfather of the celebrated Baroness Burdett-Coutts, became a partner in 1761 when Campbell died; on the death of James Coutts in 1778 Thomas Coutts took full control. Here he gained the wealth that made him the richest man in London, and which eventually made his heiress the richest woman in England. In the year 1904 Coutts's Bank moved across The Strand to No. 440, its present imposingly handsome headquarters.

Cecil House or Burleigh House, the residence of Sir William Cecil (Lord Burleigh), Queen Elizabeth's Chancellor, we have already remarked on. The Queen came to the mansion to see her Chancellor on his deathbed. John Locke was the family physician and wrote here much of his *Essay on the Human Understanding*. After Burleigh's death the mansion became Exeter House, and was pulled down in 1676.

On its site was built Exeter Change, which stood at about No. 356 Strand. On the site of Exeter Hall, at No. 372, we how have the Strand Palace Hotel, which covers the site of Haxell's Hotel and other properties, including the old *Globe* newspaper offices. In its turn Haxell's Hotel was built around the entrance of the famous old Exeter Hall, which seems to have been on the site of Bedford House (taking us back into the seventeenth century). Haxell's Hotel had an old theatrical connection, and at one time had one of the best collections of theatrical prints in London. 'Many can still remember,' wrote James Bone in 1926, 'how the boy on a cob came trotting up The Strand three times an hour with the reports from the House of Commons to the side door of the *Globe*. The *Globe* disappeared into the *Pall Mall Gazette*, and the *Pall Mall Gazette* into the *Evening Standard* into which the *St. James's Gazette* had also disappeared.'

In narrow little Exeter Street alongside, with its odd L-shape, there are never nowadays many wayfarers, though odds and ends of down-and-out humanity can often be seen there warming themselves at the blasts of hot air pouring out of the big hotel's kitchens and boiler-rooms. In this now sad and featureless little street lodged Dr Johnson when he first came to London. He stayed in the house of a stay-maker called Norris. He mentions writing part of his tragedy of *Irene* here, and also finished his poem of *London,* all in a state of grinding poverty. The poem contains the couplet:

> This mournful truth is everywhere confess'd,
> Slow rises worth by poverty depress'd.

A few yards east, and also running into The Strand from Covent Garden Market, is little Burleigh Street where, in a building still extant, the *Strand Magazine* was first printed by the house of Newnes. Soon this office was moved a few yards west to Southampton Street in a block which still pours forth many domestic magazines but no longer, alas, any *Strand.* The famous front-cover (Pl. 25), endeared to me from early childhood, offered a view along The Strand from the corner of Southampton Street. In the distance the spire of one of the famous Strand churches (St Clement Danes) peers over the shoulder of another (St Mary-le-Strand). It has been prettily said of St Mary-le-Strand that 'it swims charmingly down the Strand with St Clement Danes in its wake'.

In the middle distance of the *Strand Magazine* cover a newsboy ran across the street, and another stood on the kerb nearest to us. On the pavement on the left a young lady with a folded umbrella walked towards us, and an old gentleman with a furred collar to his coat walked away from us. A gent approached in a tall hat, and a bobby stood on the edge of the pavement. Two hansom cabs approached, one on either side of the street. This jacket was to the eyes of my infancy the quintessence of the London of my longing; and the same view is to me the quintessence of London still. Almost always this cover was a pale duck-egg shade of green, but when it came to the December (or Christmas) number it was night-time and thick snow was falling—on the same personages in the same scene—a magical transformation into winter, like that in the Christmas pantomime.

How I pored over the *Strand Magazine,* not only each month as it came out, but also over back-numbers that were printed before I had even learned to read, and which served me as picture-books in infancy. On my very first visit to London—a cheap day-trip involving two overnight journeys all the way from Glasgow and back again—almost the first thing I did was to find The Strand itself and then go to the exact spot, the base of Southampton Street, from which the magazine-cover had been originally drawn. (In strictest fact on the cover of the first few issues the point of view was from the base of Burleigh Street,

wherein the magazine was at first printed. But the necessary adjust-
ment was slight.) *Mutatis mutandis* the prospect is remarkably little
changed today. The corner building opposite is now Cook's Travel
Agency, but in the farther distance on the magazine cover we discern
a façade which is still familiar, that of Simpson's very English restaurant
on the south side of The Strand. In our own times a famous publisher
could daily be seen crossing The Strand on foot, just before one o'clock.
This was Victor Gollancz on his way to lunch at the Savoy from the
rear entrance in Maiden Lane of his office in Henrietta Street.

In the first week of 1927—my first winter in London—*The Morning
Post* left The Strand, moving east to Fleet Street. The London editor
of the *Manchester Guardian* commented :

'The paper has completed its removal from its elegant building in
The Strand to offices in Tudor Street that are very much like other
offices there. It is a little saddening to all newspaper men, for
whether one disliked its politics or not one must admit that it held,
architecturally at any rate, the prestige of the press in London. Its
granite building, designed by Messrs. Mewes and Davis, on its
island site in The Strand, always caught the eye of visitors, and it
was the only newspaper building in London which, both by its site
and its architecture, did so. . . . We shall miss the " Morning Post "
in The Strand, where it has lorded it for a century and a half.'

The newspaper did not long survive this removal.

Having reached Southampton Street in our journey down The
Strand we may linger there, and also examine its hinterland including
Maiden Lane which is at right angles, and Bedford Street which is
parallel. Southampton Street was built on the site of Bedford House,
the town house of the Earls of Bedford before they moved in 1704 to
Bedford Square. At No. 11 Sheridan's father-in-law, Thomas Linley,
the composer, died in 1795. At No. 17 Sir W. S. Gilbert, Sullivan's
partner in the Savoy Operas, was born in 1836. At No. 27 David
Garrick lived from his marriage in 1749 until 1772—the period mark-
ing the peak of his career. Somewhere in this same little street was
born Colley Cibber, actor-manager-playwright, from whose admirable
Apology for his Life I have already quoted generously. Other residents
here for a time were William Congreve, supreme Restoration comedy
writer, and Mrs Nance Oldfield, the actress, an ornament of those

same comedies; and in this same street died Dr John Lemprière, of Classical Dictionary fame. He had been both a schoolmaster and a parson, and he succumbed to apoplexy in his eightieth year.

Maiden Lane is no less distinguished in its celebrities and associations. That unsurpassed English painter, J. M. W. Turner, was born here, at No 26, in 1775 over the shop of his father who was a hairdresser and barber. The latter had some of his boy's drawings in his shop-window, hoping to sell them for a few shillings. Turner used to spend his evenings in the same street at a tavern called The Bedford Head which remained so until a very few years ago, when it became a restaurant under another name. There has been a tavern on this site since at least 1716, famous for its good fare as for its gaming. Pope and Walpole mention the Bedford Head, and Voltaire used it between 1726 and 1729 when he was resident in London. He lodged nearby, as did Andrew Marvell, probably in Southampton Street.

Pope and Walpole were Voltaire's frequent visitors and associates, usually at the Bedford Head. Here too, at No. 35, was and is Rules Restaurant, an essentially English restaurant which departs from English cuisine and service at its peril. The identity of the original Rule is unknown, but there has been a Rules since 1799. Throughout its history this has been the restaurant for journalists, actors and editors. The atmosphere is wonderfully Bohemian and informal, and is maintained by playbills, Spy cartoons, Hogarth reproductions and theatrical souvenirs. Here, recently, I looked on at a reunion of Henry Ainley's good-looking odds and ends of offspring. The legend that King Edward VII and Lillie Langtry used to sup in a *cabinet particulier* (or at least behind a violet curtain) upstairs is one that no customer would have the heart to dispute. I myself had my first memorable meal in London here in the winter of 1926, and I am still treated there by the staff and the chef with beaming respect, just as if I were one of the furnishings or one of the Spy caricatures (which indeed I practically am!). Rules takes the threat of extinction with philosophy and wit by affixing a round blue-and-white plaque: 'RULES—TO BE DEMOLISHED BY THE G.L.C. TO MAKE WAY FOR MORE ROADS AND MORE CARS.'

Maiden Lane is an odd and narrow little street, containing a Roman Catholic church, a dairy, a shop devoted to the sale of herbs and spices (until 1970) and the stage-doors or backsides of the Vaudeville and the Adelphi theatres, whose façades are in The Strand. Several cut-throat or footpad alleys communicate between Maiden Lane and The Strand. These are, from west to east, Lumley Court, Bull Inn Court and Exchange Court extending to Heathcock Court. Indeed it was in Bull Inn Court (or near the Adelphi Theatre's stage-door) that a famous actor was murdered in 1897 by a demented stage-hand with an imaginary grievance. This actor was William Terriss (Pl. 31), an Adelphi hero *par excellence*, of whom Ellen Terry said in her memoirs, writing at her divine best:

'As I look back, I remember no figure in the theatre more re-markable than Terriss. He was one of those heaven-born actors who, like kings by divine right, can, up to a certain point, do no wrong. Very often, like the "inspired idiot," Mrs Pritchard, he did not know what he was talking about. Yet he "got there", while many cleverer men stayed behind. He had unbounded impudence, yet so much charm that no one could ever be angry with him. Sometimes he reminded me of a butcher boy flashing past, whistling, on the high seat of his cart, or of Phaethon driving the chariot of the sun—pretty much the same thing, I imagine! . . . He always commanded the love of his intimates as well as that of the outside public. To the end he was "Sailor Bill"—a sort of grown-up midshipmite, whose weaknesses provoked no more condemnation than the weaknesses of a child. In the theatre he had the tidy habits of a sailor. . . . Terriss had every sort of adventure by land and sea before I acted with him at the Court. He had been midshipman, tea-planter, engineer, sheep-farmer, and horse-breeder. He had, to use his own words, "hobnobbed with every kind of queer folk, and found myself in extremely queer predicaments". The adventurous, dare-devil spirit of the roamer, the veritable gipsy, always looked out of his insolent eyes. . . . When he had presents from the front, which happened every night, he gave them at once to the call boy or the gas man. To the women-folk, especially the plainer ones, he was always delightful. Never was any man more adored by the theatre staff. . . . Perhaps if he had lived longer Terriss would have lost his throne. He died as a beautiful youth, a kind of Adonis, although he was fifty years old when he was stabbed at the stage-door of the Adelphi Theatre.'

Ellen Terry herself had so much charm as writer as well as actress that one has to force oneself to stop quoting her.

No. 21A in Maiden Lane is the site of the Cider Cellars, which was an all-night tavern famous for good eating and good cider. Rather a better class of customer was to be met here than at the Coal Hole on the other side of The Strand. Both Isaac and Benjamin Disraeli were frequenters of the Cider Cellars, and Louis Napoleon before he became Emperor of France was another frequent visitor. This resort was said to be the original of the Back Kitchen in Thackeray's *Pendennis*. A singer called Ross used to thrill such visitors with his Ballad of Sam Hall, a powerful and terrible ditty of a murderer whose catch-phrase was 'damn your eyes'. This song is still delivered on occasion, and always makes a sensation, at the 'Late Joys' in Villiers Street.

Maiden Lane runs at right angles into Bedford Street, part of which was formerly called Half-Moon Street. At No. 16 stood the house of Thomas Sheridan, the playwright's father, who was often visited there by Dr Johnson. At No. 30 was the Yorick Club, and at No. 66 was the site of the Three Tuns Tavern mentioned by Samuel Pepys. In the portion of Bedford Street between Maiden Lane and King Street were located the lodgings of Benjamin West, the American painter, and here he painted his first picture of England. Hereabouts, too, lived James Quin, a superb actor and mighty Falstaff, from 1749 to 1752. He had previously lodged near by in 1738. On the west side lived Edward Kynaston, the actor, in his old age—the odd old age of an actor who had spent his youth as an alluring female impersonator. He was long remembered and won high praise as an all-round actor from theatre writers as various as Colley Cibber and Charles Dibdin.

The portion of this street between Maiden Lane and The Strand was known as Half-Moon Street until 1766. Here was a tavern of the same name mentioned by Ned Ward in *The London Spy*. We are now in The Strand again, and may give brief consideration to the two theatres in the middle of it, both on the north side.

The first we reach after leaving Southampton Street is the Vaudeville, which has existed there since 1870, and though the auditorium has several times been rebuilt the façade is now as it always was. Here in 1891 were staged the first performances of Ibsen's *Rosmersholm* and *Hedda Gabler* for a few matinees only, the actress playing Rebecca and Hedda being Elizabeth Robins, the American player and novelist who withdrew from the stage when still young, and lived in Sussex to be nearly ninety. The Vaudeville Theatre has had two immensely long runs, one old and one comparatively recent. The first, away back in 1875, was H. J. Byron's *Our Boys*, which set up a till-then unsurpassed record for a farce of 1,362 performances. The second was a musical piece called *Salad Days*, which came from Bristol in 1954 and proceeded to run for 2,329 performances.

Between the Vaudeville and the other theatre, the Adelphi, there existed until the 1960s the celebrated Edwardian restaurant, Romano's. This was first opened by two highly successful music-hall artistes, the Sisters Leamar, with substantial assistance and backing from a stage newspaper, *The Sporting Times*, whose offices were hard by. It is a forgotten fact that the restaurant was at first called the Café Vaudeville, a name which was almost immediately changed to that of its Italian manager, Romano.

Every theatre has had its ups and downs, but the Adelphi may be said to have had rather more of both than almost any other. It opened as long ago as 1806 as the Sans Pareil, but the name was changed to the Adelphi soon afterwards in 1819. The present Adelphi is virtually the fourth new theatre on the same site. In its time it has been famous for its melodramas (just a shade more literary than those of the Lyceum), pantomimes, musical comedies and spectacles, culminating in those of Sir Charles Cochran, whose bust in bronze justly adorns the foyer. In the middle of last century the Adelphi staged many adaptations of the novels of Scott and Dickens. Throughout the eighties and nineties the Adelphi's own peculiar brand of strong drama was in vogue, plays with such titles as *The Bells of Haslemere* and *The Lights of Home*, part-author as often as not being George R. Sims. It was in one such drama, *The Trumpet Call*, that a striking dark girl was espied and reported to George Alexander as looking just right for Mrs Tanqueray in Mr Pinero's new play. This was the hitherto unknown Mrs Patrick Campbell. In Edwardian times the Adelphi vied with Daly's and the Gaiety as the home of musical comedy, with George Edwardes as general manager and Lionel Monckton as the best of a group of sparkling composers.

Besides all these considerations, The Strand, or the part of it we have now reached, is intimately and integrally connected with a strange and haunting experience of my very own. To a description of this I propose to devote the remainder of the present chapter.

On a sunny morning in June during the Second World War—the year, I believe, was 1941—I was walking down the north side of The Strand. The sky was blue and serene, but the atmosphere was sinister and chilling because there had been heavy air-raids the night before, and there came from every direction the strange sharp and jangling noise of broken window-glass being swept, shovelled and carted away in large quantities. Apart from the London County Council workmen doing this job there were very few people about, and there was very little traffic in The Strand.

Just after passing the Adelphi Theatre I was suddenly aware of an elderly lady walking, not so much slowly as with a kind of stately deliberation, in front of me (Pl. 24). My immediate reaction was that she was not entirely unfamiliar to me, that I had seen her once or twice before, walking in front of me in just such a way—once, as I remembered, in the middle of Long Acre when I lived there, and once again, as I more vaguely remembered, in that part of Oxford Street that affords a view of Derby House. As on previous occasions— two or three at most—she again struck me as a singular and remarkable old lady. But I received no impression, then or previously, that she was a hallucination or anything other-worldly. This time I resolved to have a better and more satisfying view of her, a face-to-face view, if possible, because on the previous occasions—if it *was* the same person —I had had only a glance at her features in profile. I decided to pass her swiftly, walk twenty yards or so further, look into a shop window for a few seconds, and then turn back slowly to get a full front view. From behind her, and while passing her, I could see that she was dressed, as on the previous occasions, in a black satin walking costume of a very old-fashioned style, that she had a good deal of white or cream lace around her neck, glittering earrings of what appeared to be diamonds, and a high bone-supported collarette of a kind I had not seen since my earliest infancy. I could see, too, that she was of an ashen-pale complexion—possibly powdered but with no lipstick on her mouth, which had a slight but good-natured pout. So far as I could note and remember, she wore a small black close-fitting hat of some feathery substance, and black leather shoes with what in my childhood were called Cuban heels. I had the impression, too, that the longish skirt of her costume was swathed rather than straight cut. I tried to see her hands, but both were hidden in a black or dark-brown fur muff, which was, again, out of fashion and out of season.

I passed this apparition just before reaching the façade of Coutts's Bank, a little beyond the point where Agar Street and William IV Street debouch together into The Strand below Charing Cross Hospital. After briskly walking the length of the bank, which is exactly forty of my strides (I've counted them often), I came to a halt. The first shop beyond the bank was then a tobacconist's. Stopping at this window I glanced at it for not more than a second. Then I turned to walk back and discover, without staring, what this singular lady looked like in full face. Let it be understood that I had lost sight of her for rather less than thirty seconds.

To my profound surprise I found, on looking round and turning back, that the old lady had utterly vanished. There was not a living soul in front of me for the whole length of Coutts's Bank. She was not crossing The Strand and there was no one in the least like her on the opposite side. It was just, but barely, possible that she had suddenly hailed a taxi and driven off in it. But no taxi or car was in sight in either direction. Why, then, she must have gone into the bank itself, which again was possible, since she ought to have been very close to the bank's front door at the moment when I turned round to have a good look.

It was just on the stroke of ten o'clock, the bank's opening time. When I reached the front door a commissionaire was in process of throwing the doors open. Much perplexed if not exactly astonished I said to him: 'Good morning, has a lady dressed in black just come in?' He smiled and said: 'How could she, sir, I have just this second opened the door?' There was nothing to do except to thank him and to come away mystified and far from satisfied. But I still thought of my old lady as an inexplicable and not as a ghostly or supernatural apparition.

Less than a week afterwards I found myself describing this odd experience to the landlord of the Bird in Hand in Long Acre, Arthur Powell. I had not quite finished telling my story when he interrupted me. He had been listening intently, watching me closely and gravely and without the usual twinkle in his eyes. Also he was without the usual sceptical smile of a listener who suspects one to be 'spinning a yarn'. He said: 'I know who it was you saw, or think you saw. It was the Baroness Burdett-Coutts. I recognized her from your description of her. You saw her vanishing into her own bank!' I gasped and expostulated. Surely the Baroness died forty years ago at least? And in any case how did this pub landlord recognize such a person merely from my vague description? He said very firmly and still unsmilingly: 'Of course I recognized her. I saw her quite often in the old days. You see, my father was one of her coachmen.'

At this juncture some other customers came into the tavern and the spell of strangeness was temporarily suspended. But it was not completely broken, and it asserted itself again in several subsequent conversations in which the old Welshman repeated his conviction that it was none other than the Baroness I had seen, or thought I had seen. At this time I happened to know very little about the Baroness Burdett-Coutts—not even that she was directly concerned with Coutts's Bank. As a Dickens lover I had known that she was a great friend of Charles Dickens in her middle age, and as a drama critic and theatre lover I knew, too, that she was a helpful friend of Henry Irving in her old age and that she was reported to have financed some of his last theatrical ventures at the Lyceum. Also that she had lent her great house in Piccadilly for the celebrated actor's lying-in-state. Sir Henry Irving died in October 1905, and it is not entirely irrelevant to add here that I myself was born in January of that same year.

In 1953 a biography of the Baroness appeared. Entitled *Angela Burdett-Coutts and the Victorians*, it was written by the Hon. Mrs Clara Burdett Patterson, the Baroness's great-niece. It need hardly be said that I read this book eagerly and also reviewed it. Before I read a word of it, however, I studied closely the portraits of the Baroness at various ages which illustrate the book. The first is a head-and-shoulders portrait of the girl, Angela Burdett (born 1814), whose earliest recollection was of having a very old lady pointed out to her at Brighton as being Mrs Piozzi, formerly Mrs Thrale. If my ghost be genuine—and I have hardly any reason to doubt it—I have more than once set eyes on a lady who as a child glimpsed Mrs Thrale, who had in her day been one of the dearest woman friends of Dr Johnson himself!

The second portrait in the book was of Angela Burdett-Coutts in her early thirties, a most elegant full-length and full-dress likeness, painted by W. C. Ross in water-colour on ivory. This, the more I study it, is the portrait most uncannily like my apparition. The face is in three-quarter profile. The third portrait in the book, again full length and again in full court dress, was painted by Edwin Long and still, I believe, hangs in the Burdett-Coutts Schools in Westminster. It emphasizes the lady's considerable height—a feature which I especially noted in her apparition—and her corresponding leanness.

The last picture, once again full length, is a drawing of the Baroness as a bride, on the arm of her bridegroom and with an officiating clergyman between the heads of the old-young couple. There was a disparity in age of exactly forty years. This wedding shocked Queen Victoria, who had until then favoured the Baroness with her friendship and used often to sit on the latter's balcony watching the endless traffic in Piccadilly. Only there, the Queen would say, could she watch the London traffic without it stopping on her account. But after the wedding those royal visits were discontinued, and the Baroness was invited to Buckingham Palace only on formal occasions.

This is not the place or the occasion to give more than a sketch of this remarkable lady's career. But her family history is of quite exceptional interest even before she was born in 1814, the year before the battle of Waterloo. Her grandfather, the banker Thomas Coutts, married his brother's maidservant and by her had three daughters, all of whom made brilliant matches. The eldest, Fanny, married the Marquess of Bute; the second, Susan, married Lord Guildford; and the third, Sophia, married Sir Francis Burdett, who was to be Angela's father.

For four years before her death Thomas Coutts's first wife suffered from mental collapse and ceased to be in any sense a companion to him. Some time before her death the old man, when over seventy, had fallen in love with the actress Harriot Mellon, then about forty; and in 1815 he married her, exactly a fortnight after his wife's death.

The three titled daughters were now torn between love of their father and extreme dislike of his second marriage to a woman whom they deemed a vulgarian. After much family quarrelling and disagreement, the old man, who seems to have had a dash of King Lear about him as well as a dash of Balzac's Père Goriot, came to live with his youngest daughter and her husband (the Burdetts) in his own Piccadilly mansion.

When old Thomas Coutts died in 1822 it was found that he had left the whole of his great fortune to his wife, Harriot. There was much adverse comment on this, but his three daughters had been well provided for already. Harriot Coutts remained a widow for five years, and at the end of that period married William Aubrey de Vere, ninth Duke of St Albans, who was some twenty-five years her junior. He had to ask her three times before she consented.

After her marriage the Duchess of St Albans wrote an admirable letter to Sir Walter Scott in answer to one of his which has not been

preserved. The Duchess's letter is still to be seen at Abbotsford:
'Thanks, many thanks for all your kind congratulations. I am a
Duchess at last, that is certain, but whether I am the better for it
remains to be proved. The Duke is very amiable, gentle and well-
disposed, and I am sure he has taken pains enough to accomplish what
he says has been the first wish of his heart for the last three years. All
this is very flattering to an old lady, and we lived so long in friendship
with each other that I should be unhappy if I did not say I *will*—yet
the name of Coutts—and a right good one it is—is, and ever will be,
dear to my heart.' She goes on rather touchingly to comment on her
own career, with a slight misquotation to indicate that she had once
been Ophelia in her play-acting days:

'What a strange, eventful life mine has been, from a poor little
player child, with just food and clothes to cover me, dependent on
a very precarious profession, without talent or a friend in the world
"to have seen what I have seen, seeing what I see". Is it not
wonderful? Is it true? Can I believe it?—first the wife of the best,
the most perfect being that ever breathed, his immense fortune so
honourably acquired by his own industry, all at my command . . .
and now the wife of a Duke. You must write my life; the History of
Tom Thumb, Jack the Giant Killer, and Goody Two Shoes will
sink compared to my true history written by the author of *Waverley*,
and that you may do it well I have sent you an inkstand. Pray give
it a place on your table in kind remembrance of your affectionate
friend.'

To this day the Duchess of St Albans's inkstand is to be gazed upon at
Abbotsford.

She died in 1837, and to universal astonishment left the whole of the
huge Coutts fortune to her husband's granddaughter, Angela Burdett.
Here I quote Mrs Patterson: 'It appeared that Harriot had taken a
great fancy to Angela, who, as is sometimes the way of children of a
younger generation, had ignored the family differences and had found
pleasure in the kind company of the woman who, after all, must have
possessed many endearing attributes.'

The Duke, her husband, had died leaving her childless, and she
made the young Angela Burdett her regular travelling companion.
Incidentally, the Duchess travelled in very great state, usually in a
cavalcade of coaches with a small army of servants and couriers, with

two doctors in attendance (in case one of them fell ill), and with two chambermaids (one for day and one for night duty) for the highly interesting reason that she was afraid of ghosts and could not bear ever to be alone, night or day.

The Duchess's will was signed only a fortnight before her death, and young Angela Burdett found herself in the possession of a fortune of approximately £80,000 a year. Simultaneously she became a national celebrity, a popular byword for a rich heiress, with a complimentary mention in the Rev. Richard Barham's *Ingoldsby Legends*, which first appeared in volume form in 1840. Again let me quote her great-niece and biographer: 'I think that during the long talks which Angela probably had with her step-grandmother, especially on their interminable drives, the old lady, who herself had no easy youth, must have instilled into her husband's youngest granddaughter a deep concern for the trials and sufferings of others; or at all events she must have discovered in Angela a sympathy and large-heartedness which could easily be encouraged. . . .'

Almost from the start she encouraged it in herself: 'Angela was occupied at first with her social life, entertaining and being entertained; and gradually, as time went on, occupied herself more and more with her charities and with business affairs, as she had inherited some of the shrewdness and far-seeing qualities of her grandfather, Thomas Coutts. She was one of the first to perceive that the day of private banking firms was over, and the fact that the great business of Coutts was turned into an unlimited private joint stock company was chiefly due to her foresight and influence.'

From the start the heiress was naturally besieged by suitors. With the aid of her regular maid-companion, Miss Meredith, she learned how to dispose of these: 'Miss Meredith became quite expert at seeing that a proposal was coming, and on these occasions retired to the adjoining room, leaving the door open. When the proposal had taken place, Angela would give a cough, and Miss Meredith would at once return to relieve an awkward situation. Lord Houghton once said that he believed Miss Coutts liked him because he had never proposed to her.'

Miss Meredith, in short, acted as Nerissa to this Portia, this 'lady richly left'. But the lady was a Portia who, in spite of her sense of fun, retained her dignity. Her achievements were chiefly charitable and philanthropic. Few wealthy persons have ever put their money to so much good use, or used so much imaginative foresight in so doing. I have already mentioned Charles Dickens and Henry Irving as being two close friends who taught her to conserve her wealth even while she distributed a large amount of it in charity. An earlier and even closer friend was the great Duke of Wellington. At one time it was commonly stated that she intended to marry him, though he was old enough to be her grandfather. They gave up the idea of marrying early in 1847 when Angela was thirty-three and the Duke of Wellington was nearly seventy-eight. In a letter which has been preserved he advises her not to throw herself away upon a man so much her senior, and she took his advice. She lived for nearly another sixty years after that letter was written, pestered by a crowd of beggars but untouched by scandal.

In the year 1871 the State acknowledged this lady's manifold charities by giving her a peerage—the first woman in England to be so honoured for her own deeds and merits. In the following year she was given the freedom of the City of London.

In 1881 the Baroness, then sixty-seven, married a man exactly forty years younger. He was William Ashmead-Bartlett, an American who had been her secretary; and the marriage threw a bombshell into English Society. Queen Victoria, as we have seen, was so little amused that she called the Baroness a 'silly old woman'. But the biographer writes from her own experience:

'I only knew them both when she was an aged woman and he was a man between forty and fifty with greying hair, but she still adored him. As far as one can tell, she, at any rate, was happy during the twenty-six years of their married life. She always addressed him with utmost affection. Once at Holly Lodge [her country house] I saw her remove her wedding ring from her finger for some reason. Presently she turned to her husband and said, "No one but you shall put it on again, Ashmead," and he replaced it on her finger with the courtesy with which I always saw him treat her.'

The amazing marriage took place at Christ Church, Down Street, Piccadilly, a church which the Baroness herself had endowed. Her biographer notes: 'Just as in the case of many a younger woman, marriage softened the Baroness, gave her a wider and more understanding outlook with regard to individual relationships, attributes which so far had been reserved mostly for humanity as a whole.' In the year after the marriage the bridegroom assumed the bride's name of Burdett-Coutts and dropped his own. Another year later he stood for Parliament and was elected Conservative member for Westminster. He survived the Baroness, living on until 1922.

Sir Henry Irving, as I have said, died in October 1905, and the Baroness, knowing that his flat in Grafton Street was much too small for the purpose, placed her house at the disposal of his kindred. The great actor lay in state in her large dining-room. Over his heart was laid a cross of flowers from Queen Alexandra, and on a table beside the coffin was a wreath from Ellen Terry. A procession of mourners moved round the coffin all the day from dawn till dusk.

The Baroness Burdett-Coutts followed Irving to Westminster Abbey little more than a year later. She died at the great age of ninety-two on 30th December 1906. King Edward VII said of her that she was 'after my mother the most remarkable woman in the kingdom'. The amount of good that she did with her great fortune is incalculable.

And now here am I, born in the year of Irving's death, fully convinced that I have seen the tangible spirit of Baroness Burdett-Coutts in her habit as she lived, and who yet died and was buried in Westminster Abbey when I was a two-year-old. I have told my tale *viva voce* to some of her descendants—Mrs Patterson's daughter and her husband—and with no more elaboration or adornment than I have given it here. They had no sceptical look in their eyes as I did so. They said, in fact, that it was by no means the first rumour they had heard of their distinguished ancestor being seen on an unattended walk in the streets of London. She had been reported as having been seen not only in the West End but also in the East End, where she endowed a market and a block of model dwelling-houses in Bethnal Green.

Shall I encounter her again? I fervently and eagerly hope so, and never walk up or down The Strand, which I do often, without thinking of her and seeing her again vividly, but, alas, only in the mind's eye. And next time the apparition does meet my actual gaze I shall 'cross it though it blast me', as Horatio said of the ghost of Hamlet's father. I shall say 'Good morning, Baroness', and see what happens.

CHAPTER SIX

ST MARTIN'S—CHURCH AND LANE

In the middle thirties a Continental architect, Paul Cohen-Portheim, produced a book called *The Spirit of London*, which is still valuable as showing the city from the point of view of an outsider. He is particularly interesting on The Strand itself when he writes:

'The Strand has continuously changed its aspect. A generation ago [meaning at the turn of the century] it was still the centre of London's theatre and night life, its "boulevard", but now that life has moved further west. Instead The Strand is becoming an "Empire" street. The houses of the British Commonwealth are here, Canada and South Africa in Trafalgar Square, Australia and New Zealand in The Strand, India just behind it. The Strand is London's great Overseas street. It stands for "dear old London" to the exiles, who have bought their tropical outfits in its shops, even if there is little left that can be called old. It is one of the most alive streets of London, not quite the City yet, but leading up to it. It is a man's street, a City-rush street, also a tourists' street. One has a feeling that the people one passes have just come back from Rhodesia or are just off to Singapore; and it is always full of men who look a little lost, as if they did not quite know their way about.'

This foreign observer's chief point would appear to be that The Strand is too full of visitors and travellers and too short of Londoners to be a characteristic London street. But to me, and thousands like me, The Strand is the very core of London, just as the famous old *Strand Magazine* cover is the very core of The Strand. Another eloquent lover of London, E. V. Lucas, admits this in a famous passage in which he tries to explain his own antipathy to the thoroughfare that culminates at one end in Fleet Street and at the other in Trafalgar Square: 'I could not, I think, explain why, but I have more distaste for The

Strand than for any street in London. I would avoid it as carefully, from pure unreasoning prejudice, as Count D'Orsay or Dick Swiveller avoided certain other districts on financial grounds. This, I fear, proves me to be only half a Londoner—if that; for The Strand to many people *is* London, all else being extraneous. They endure their daily tasks elsewhere only because such endurance provides them with the means to be in The Strand at night.'

This passage, in a writer whom I find in every other respect so congenial, I utterly fail to understand. For twenty years of my life I lived within a furlong of The Strand, and it is for me haunted with figures of the past as well as persons of the present. I have already described a very eminent ghost I actually encountered there. There are at least three other ghosts—all of literary men—whom it would not profoundly surprise me to run up against in this part of London, in the intangible flesh. Two of them are, as almost goes without saying, Boswell and Johnson. I never traverse any of the numerous alleys between The Strand and Long Acre without envisaging Jamie Boswell bent on undignified pleasures and all but slavering with anticipated delights. I think often of Johnson, too, in this neighbourhood, and particularly recall a strange view of him in Samuel Whyte's *Miscellanea Nova*. Whyte was a friend of Thomas Sheridan who lived in Bedford Street, facing Henrietta Street and the south side of Covent Garden:

'One day we were standing together at the drawing-room window expecting Johnson, who was to dine with us. Mr. Sheridan asked me could I see the length of the garden. "No, sir." "Take out your opera-glass then: Johnson is coming, you may know him by his gait." I perceived him at a good distance, walking along with a peculiar solemnity of deportment, and an awkward, measured sort of step. At that time the broad flagging at each side of the streets was not universally adopted, and stone posts were in fashion to prevent the annoyance of carriages. Upon every post, as he passed along, I could observe he deliberately laid his hand; but missing one of them, when he had got to some distance he seemed suddenly to recollect himself, and immediately returning back, carefully performed the accustomed ceremony, and resumed his former course, not omitting one, till he gained the crossing. This, Mr. Sheridan assured me, however odd it might appear, was his constant practice, but why or wherefore he could not inform me.'

This eccentric habit of Johnson, the result of hypochondriacal nervousness or a 'fixation', is also described by Boswell, but much less vividly, meseems, or as a thing more taken for granted.

Another ghost who must be around, though it has never been my luck to see him, is John Hollingshead (Pl. 26), who was born in 1827 and died at Fulham in 1904, the year before I was born. Hollingshead was born in Hoxton and as a child he saw something of Charles Lamb. A relation of his had been the nurse of Mary Lamb during her last six years. After an unsuccessful start in business Hollingshead became a journalist. He is said to have known both Hazlitt and William Godwin. He sent a contribution to *Household Words*—it was then edited by Charles Dickens—and he at once joined the staff and contributed many articles of city life and a description of the Sayers-Heenan fight. He was also one of the first contributors to the *Cornhill Magazine*, which first appeared in 1859. When Thackeray, the editor, asked where he had learned his pure style of writing, he replied: 'In the streets, from costermongers and skittle-yards.' In the 'sixties he acted as successor to Edmund Yates, dramatic critic of *The Daily News*. As an occasional contributor to *Punch* he pleaded—with effective satire—for improvements in the government of London. Here he especially attacked the Duke of Bedford, whom he christened the Duke of Mudford, on account of his mismanagement of the Covent Garden property. Two articles of Hollingshead's entitled 'Mud Salad Market' and 'The Gates of Gloomsbury' attracted wide and general attention. By 'Mud Salad' he meant, of course, Covent Garden.

He took a spirited part in other public movements. With the actor-playwright Dion Boucicault he agitated in favour of 'Free Trade for Theatres' and against the licensing regulations. He was a man who knew how to effect changes for the better, a great righter of wrongs. In 1873 he succeeded in reforming the copyright laws so as to prevent the dramatization of novels without the author's permission or advantage. In this matter he was Charles Dickens's especial friend and helpmate. He helped to found the Arundel Club and the New Club in Covent Garden. He became a real Covent Garden Bohemian.

In 1865 he took up theatrical management for the first time and persisted in it until his death. He continued at the same time to be a journalist, though less regularly. Till 1868 he was stage-director of the Alhambra. Just before Christmas 1868 he began as manager of the newly built Gaiety Theatre in The Strand. Here in this long-successful house Hollingshead inaugurated the system of mid-week and Saturday matinees. He was also the first to use electric illumination outside the theatre, and shortly afterwards made use of it on the stage as well. As already recounted, his chief interest was in burlesque, an earlier and more satirical form of musical comedy. But Hollingshead also had serious plays in his theatre: his playwrights including W. S. Gilbert, Charles Reade, H. J. Byron, and Dion Boucicault. He staged opera with such singers as Charles Santley. He even staged Shakespeare as well as old and modern English comedy with such actors as J. L. Toole, Samuel Phelps and Charles Mathews, and later Forbes-Robertson, Ada Cavendish, Mrs John Wood and Rose Leclercq. It was here, also, in 1871 that Hollingshead staged the very first Gilbert and Sullivan opera, *Thespis: or the Palace of Truth*; and London's very first Ibsen production, a translation by William Archer of *The Pillars of Society* which the translator called *Quicksands*. ('A worthy pioneer!' as Hamlet so mysteriously says of the Ghost.) The Ibsen presentation was in 1880. Hollingshead did even more than that. It has been said of him that with great public spirit, benevolence and success he organized many benefits for old actors or public objects. He was in these matters like no one so much as Charles B. Cochran in our own time. It was Hollingshead, for example, who arranged for the complete company of the Comédie Française to give a six-weeks' season (forty-two performances in all) in the mid summer of 1879. The season was a commercial and cultural triumph. The company included Sarah Bernhardt, Got, Delaunay, the two Coquelins, Febvre and Mounet-Sully.

In 1888 Hollingshead resigned the management of the Gaiety to George Edwardes. He had been a successful but also a generous manager for eighteen years. An able agitator, he led the public protest against the erection of the railway bridge over Ludgate Circus. But the bridge was duly erected, and is still there! In his later years he lost the Gaiety fortune in music-hall speculations. He died in his house in Fulham Road and was buried in Brompton Cemetery near Sir Augustus Harris and Nelly Farren. He had published many books of reminiscences and books made up of old articles, including in 1892 *The Story of Leicester Square*. But these days he is too much forgotten and ignored. His ghost should walk—and probably does.

We have now in the course of our perambulation of The Strand come close to Charing Cross itself, and we turn along short Duncannon Street to reach Trafalgar Square and the façade of the world-famous church of St Martin (Pl. 29). As a result of Nash opening up the great Square in 1829, the church of St Martin-in-the-Fields suddenly became one of the most handsomely situated of all London's old buildings. The fields of the church's title were all round it originally, and were the property of Westminster Abbey. The original church was a small chapel in the twelfth century. In the middle of the sixteenth century this was rebuilt, but was still very small. In the next two hundred years it grew piecemeal, and its tower received a cupola designed by Sir Christopher Wren. By this time it was accepted as the church of the Royal Parish; several royal babies, including the little prince who was to become King Charles II, were christened in it. Queen Mary I worshipped there, and when James Gibbs (Pl. 30) built the handsome new church, which is today's handsome old one, King George I presented it with its organ. There was a royal pew provided, complete with fireplace. These things explain why the Royal Coat of Arms is conspicuous on the pediment. In the church and its graveyard a very remarkable variety of notables lie buried. They include Nicholas Hilliard, George Farquhar, Francis Bacon, Nell Gwynne, John Hampden, Jack Sheppard the thief and escapologist, Nicholas Stone the sculptor and his son of the same name and persuasion, and the judge, Sir Edmundbury Godfrey, who was found murdered on Primrose Hill—a crime alleged to have been committed by the desperate associates of Titus Oates. It should be noted that the graveyard of St Martin's was where the National Gallery now stands, on the north side of Trafalgar Square.

Gibbs built this church, his best-known work, between 1722 and 1726, when he was in his early forties. He was from Aberdeenshire, a Scot whom the Scots have forgotten to honour, perhaps because his best work was done in London. He studied architecture in Holland and in Rome. His first public building in London was the church of St Mary-le-Strand, as we have already noted. This was consecrated in 1723. He added the steeple and the two upper stages to Wren's church of St Clement Danes, a few yards farther east. In June of 1722 he began another fine building, the Senate House at Cambridge. He designed several of the noblest monuments in Westminster Abbey, including that to Ben Jonson; planned and brought off the breathtaking beauty of the new wing of King's College, Cambridge; designed the stately quadrangle of St Bartholomew's Hospital in London; and erected the Radcliffe Library at Oxford, a thing outstanding even in that city of noble edifices.

Gibbs was also the author and the translator of treatises on architecture which are studied still. But in spite of all those accomplishments and achievements, or partly because of them, he is an architect without honour in his own country. Horace Walpole said that his designs wanted 'the harmonious simplicity of the greatest masters of architecture'. Yet this criticism is now declared to be less than his due, and he is today generally regarded as perhaps the most considerable master of British architecture since Sir Christopher Wren. But not by all.

The most modern critics of the art say of St Martin's Church: 'Gibbs had built it closely confined in its Lane, had perhaps thought of the temple portico as seen only from close to and its spire as riding not the portico but the surrounding rooftops. Certainly he had regretted not having his earlier design for a circular church accepted. But, whatever allowances we make, the way the spire rides the temple is absurd, the interrupted string-course and rusticated window surrounds are ungraceful and inappropriate; and the east front, the flattest aspect of the church, is by far the most satisfactory.'

It seems that Gibbs studied for the Catholic priesthood when in Rome, and that he later joined the Church of England when in London. The same writers just quoted think that this indecision is reflected in his design for St Martin's Church: 'It shews how difficult he found it to solve the problem of combining Roman architecture and Anglican liturgy. The interior of St. Mary-le-Strand is a mere echo of its distinctive and charmingly Roman exterior. At St. Martin's, as it was originally built, the nave moves slowly East, turns handsomely into the chancel arch, and then has nowhere to go: no splendid baldaquin, no flamboyantly emotional altar. The royal arms symbolically cut off that part of the church most important to a Catholic.' Such architectural criticism is to me as inscrutable as some modern architecture. Myself I miss neither the 'splendid baldaquin' nor the 'flamboyantly emotional altar'. It seems to my admittedly not very architectural way of seeing things that Gibbs is quite right to be neither too fancy nor too plain, neither too Catholic nor too Anglican, in this particular building. It seems to me, also, that he had an exact knowledge of his own intentions. He himself wrote of this church: 'The ceiling is ellyptical, which, I find by experience, to be much better for the voice than the semicircular, tho' not so beautiful.' But it is fair to complete the modern critical viewpoint and comment on this statement: 'This is *like* Gibbs; he could never quite make a virtue of necessity, make the imaginative leap which turns the theoretically inadequate or outrageous into an individual, a unique beauty. Parts, one might say, excellent; synthesis weak.'

This examination concludes by allowing Gibbs's published drawings, particularly of St Martin's, to have had a great influence in the eighteenth century both in England and in the United States. When I visited Georgia and South Carolina in the winter of 1953, I remember gazing on certain handsome churches in both Savannah and Charleston, dominating their own little eighteenth-century squares, and murmuring to myself 'How like James Gibbs!' hardly aware of how perceptive I was being. Moreover I never look on the western façade of this particularly endeared London church, usually from the steps of the National Gallery, without thinking how intensely satisfying it looks from there, just as James Tissot painted it in the cool clear light of a showery spring morning.

For one onlooker at least there is nothing in the least absurd in 'the way the spire rides the temple', nor am I able to see anything ungraceful and inappropriate in the 'rusticated window surrounds'. Sir John Summerson criticizes St Martin's with far more affection and forbearance: 'No amount of skill can ever make a happy marriage between a portico and a tower, when the latter is set on top of the former, though it is very remarkable how determined English architects have been to try. The tower, of course, does not really ride on the pitched roof and this important fact must, somehow or other, be expressed.'

When I visit the church, I think of the many friends and associates whose memorial services I have attended here. I remember well and with awe how nobly Henry Ainley, looking like an archangel in ruins, spoke at the service (1939) for the actor Sir Frank Benson, in whose company he was trained. On another such occasion, for Marie Tempest in 1942, the sadness was slightly marred by the sudden appearance in the seat in front of me of two ripe comedians who came in together— Alfred Drayton and Robertson Hare. (Popular comedians should not attend such occasions at all—or not, at least, together.) The service for Henry Ainley himself (in November 1945) was a darkling occasion, which made my old mentor James Agate look back on the actor's career in a retrospective essay and come to a lasting conclusion:

'I blame Nature for having given this near-great actor too much and not enough. For having lavished on him a combination and a form which automatically brought up Hamlet's description of his father, to which was added a voice like a cathedral organ. For having drawn back her hand and given a man physically endowed to play tragedy the instincts of the comedian. Ainley was almost the worst Hamlet and quite the worst Macbeth I have ever seen. Such was the tragedian. About Ainley the comedian I did not see quite enough to make up my mind. I never saw the play called *Quinneys*'. In *The Great Adventure* he seemed to me to be admirable in the first act but too big for the rest of the play. I missed, alas, his Benedick.'

Among those comic performances I saw *The Great Adventure* only as a silent film, and even so thought Ainley's performance a masterpiece of personal charm throughout, and that the performance as a whole was no whit bigger or smaller than the Arnold Bennett play itself. I think, too, that James was foolish to miss the Benedick, which was again compact of charm and the pluter-perfect delivery of Shakespeare's prose. The truth is that J.A. was at his best about Ainley when Ainley himself was at his best. See his notice of the actor as the Archangel in Bridie's *Tobias and the Angel*: 'Mr. Ainley acts superbly throughout. His assumption of common humanity is very well done, and he is not afraid of diminishing his Angel by the use of irony and even fun. He looks magnificent whether in rags, golden mail, or ultimate white. When in the last scene he stands pedestalled and remote from the reunited family he seems more than life-size.'

Then, in 1950, there was the harrowing Service at St Martin's for Sir Frederick Bain, 'a kinder friend had no man', who in the course of our long friendship gave me the courtesy of a father and the benevolence of the best kind of uncle. At the Service in 1958 for Robert Donat, a fine romantic actor who died too young, they played a tape-recording found in the actor's bedroom after his death, and whereon he had recorded a prayer of St Francis, ending thus nobly:

> For it is by giving that one receives,
> It is by self-forgetting that one finds,
> It is by forgiving that one is forgiven,
> It is by dying that one awakens to eternal life.

At another (1960), for George Relph, a modest but most expressive actor, Sir Ralph Richardson read the lesson, and Sir Laurence Olivier gave the address. At yet another (1965), for George Bishop, one of my very first friends in journalism, a supreme craftsman among theatrical commentators, it was very rightly said, as was said of Hardy's Giles Winterborne, that 'he was a good man and did good things'.

I was present likewise in 1966 at the Service for C. S. Forester the novelist. I did not know him well, but I had stayed as a guest at his home in Berkeley, California, for a memorable week in 1953. I best remember him for his gentleness and for his habit of playing Sullivan comic-opera tunes on a tin-whistle alone in his room in the early morning. And finally there was the endeared and brilliant Vivien Leigh for whose Service, in August 1967, all the best actors in England assembled and were most movingly addressed by Sir John Gielgud who had us all—and not least himself—in tears. The tablet to her memory bears the words from *Antony and Cleopatra*:

> Now boast thee death, in thy possession lies
> A lass unparallel'd.

I have, I suppose, attended other memorial services at St Martin-in-the-Fields. But those are the ones I best recall, and I never pass the church without recollecting some of the great ones who have made my life in London so rich and treasurable in memory.

St Martin's Lane (Pl. 29) was built around the year 1613 and was at first called West Church Lane; as late as 1658 it was the western boundary of the town. It can be seen from old maps that this street ran right down to The Strand in the days before Trafalgar Square was built (in the early nineteenth century). This explains the oddity of the street-numbering which begins at No. 30 (around the Chandos Tavern on the south-east corner), continues by single numbers to No 70 at the corner of Garrick Street, and is continued on the west side from No. 74 or so right down to No. 120 or so, a bank at the corner of St Martin's Place. Let us begin at the north-west corner.

Renault's spacious car show-room now occupies the site of Old Slaughter's coffee-house at the corner of St Martin's Lane and Cranbourn Street. Before extensive alterations were carried out in 1970, an elegant but inconspicuous plaque could have been seen there. It

was surmounted by a frieze showing four club-members grouped round
a table above the wording

NEAR THIS SPOT STOOD OLD SLAUGHTER'S
COFFEE HOUSE, WHERE IN 1824 WAS
FORMED THE FIRST ANIMAL PROTECTION
SOCIETY TO BE FOUNDED IN ANY COUNTRY,
NOW KNOWN AS THE
ROYAL SOCIETY FOR THE PREVENTION
OF CRUELTY TO ANIMALS

PRESENT HEADQUARTERS: 105 JERMYN STREET, LONDON S.W.I.

Before this laudable society existed, here stood Old Slaughter's itself,
from 1692 till 1824. It was the great haunt of artists ranging from
William Hogarth to David Wilkie. That fine painter, Richard Wilson,
neglected and almost starved by the art patrons of his day, occasionally
came to Slaughter's to meet his countryman, blind John Parry, the
Welsh harpist. Parry played his harp to Thomas Gray, the poet, at
Cambridge, and Gray in a letter dated 1757 says that he 'scratched out
such a ravishing blind harmony, such tunes of a thousand years old',
but he 'put my Ode [*The Bard*] in motion again, and has brought it
at last to a conclusion'.

New Slaughter's (at No 82 in 1828) was established about 1760,
and was demolished in 1843 when 'the new avenue of Garrick Street'
was made. It was much frequented by artists in search of cheap fare
and good society—such as Wilkie, who was always the last dropper-in
and was never seen to dine in the house before dark. The truth is that
that patient young Scotsman always slaved at his art till the last
glimpse of daylight had faded from the city's skies.

Hogarth's father-in-law Sir James Thornhill, who painted the great
ceiling in the banqueting hall at Greenwich Naval College, lived at
104 St Martin's Lane. Thereafter there dwelt in the same house
Francis Hayman, who decorated Vauxhall and illustrated countless
books, and whose pictures were sometimes good enough to be mistaken
for Hogarth's own. He was a boon companion of Hogarth, and also of
the actors Garrick, Quin and Woodward.

At No. 31 Inigo Jones was said to have built himself a house. At No.
60 on the same side the famous furniture-maker Thomas Chippendale

had his first workshop, and published *The Gentleman and Cabinet Maker's Director*. Near by, quite recently, was the workshop of the firm of Motley, a group of ladies who became one of the most tasteful and inventive stage-designers and costumiers of our time. At No. 70 lived Nathaniel Hone, the miniature-painter, around 1775.

Josiah Wedgwood's residence and show-rooms were at the corner of Newport Street in a house demolished when Cranbourn Street was built. Between 1768 and 1774 the roadway was frequently blocked by the carriages of his visitors. At No. 82 is the Westminster County Court which is on the site of New Slaughter's Coffee House. Here met a famous scientific society that included Sir Joseph Banks, the founder of Kew Gardens, Captain Cook the explorer, Dr Solander, the natural historian who had a goose named after him, John Smeaton, the bridge and lighthouse builder, and Jesse Ramsden, who made telescopes. John Hunter, the great Scottish surgeon, was its chairman.

At No. 88–9 lived John Pine, the engraver, and at No. 34, in Burleigh Mansions alongside, lived Ellen Terry for a time when she was Mrs James Carew. At No. 100 dwelt the eccentric painter Henry Fuseli between 1779 and 1784 when he married a Miss Rawlins and thereafter moved to Foley Street.

The earliest theatre to be erected in St Martin's Lane was the Duke of York's, originally called the Trafalgar (built in 1892). The American actress Elizabeth Robins was giving Ibsen matinees there at the time when she handed over the part of Mrs Tanqueray to a complete new-comer, Mrs Patrick Campbell. The latter was to make her first sensational success in this part, whereas the talented Miss Robins never made a sensational success in anything. Charles Frohman, the American manager who was later to drown in the *Lusitania* (in 1915), took a long lease of this theatre in 1897, and in the course of his seasons some of Barrie's plays were seen for the first time. Here, for example, opened *Peter Pan* on 27th December 1904, a date preceding by exactly ten days the birthday of another Boy Who Never Grew Up—myself.

When I came to be a practising dramatic critic, and even after I desisted (in 1960), no play at this theatre gave me more pleasure than Noël Coward's *Waiting in the Wings* which opened in September 1960 and ran for only a few months. It was killed by a savage manhandling in some of the cheaper London dailies. This was, despite their opinions, a good play.

Still on the west side of St Martin's Lane, at Nos 110 and 111, and between the two theatres, was Peter's Court where Louis François Roubillac had his first London studio. This sculptor, a native of Lyons, came to England around 1738. He executed many busts and statues of such celebrities as Shakespeare, Handel and Hogarth; his bust of Sir Isaac Newton at Cambridge is none the worse for looking like Laurence Olivier skilfully made up as the discoverer of the force of gravity. Roubillac was a friendly, talkative, gesticulating little man who even after thirty years in England retained his strong foreign accent. He was buried in the graveyard of St Martin's Church 'under the window of Bell Bagnio', whatever that may signify. His rooms were eventually occupied by Hogarth who founded there the St Martin's Academy which was the forerunner of the Royal Academy. At No. 114 was the residence of the first Earl of Shaftesbury from 1675 to 1677. It is on record that Ben Jonson went to a private school in St Martin's Lane. Hereabouts, too, lived Dr Thomas Tenison, rector of St Martin's and later (1694–1715) Archbishop of Canterbury. The Dutch painter Daniel Mytens flourished in this street from 1622 to 1634. Being portrait-painter to both James I and Charles I he became known as the King's Painter. He was unconventional and positively impressionist in technique, and there is an exciting self-portrait of him at Hampton Court. He learned his craft in Rubens's studio at Antwerp.

That arch man-of-the-world, Sir Kenelm Digby, and also Sir John Suckling (Millamant's 'natural, easy Suckling' and John Aubrey's 'extraordinary accomplished Gent') were residing in St Martin's Lane in 1641. Sir Henry Wotton when Provost of Eton had his London lodging in this street. Scholar, diplomat and friend of Donne, Wotton is one of the least ignorable—and most ignored—of the Elizabethans. He never lived down the reputation of being a great liar, largely due to his having once (according to Izaak Walton) included himself in the definition—'An ambassador is an honest man, sent to lie abroad for the good of his country.' Wotton returned penniless to England after ambassadorial duties in Europe (1624), but was soon enrolled as Provost of Eton. He was a dilettante, an educator, an angler and generally a man of amiable parts. But his best claim to eternal fame is his poetry, a little of which Palgrave perpetuated in his *Golden Treasury*—'The Character of a Happy Life', and 'On His Mistress, the Queen of Bohemia'.

William Dobson, the portrait-painter and protégé of Van Dyck, died in poverty in St Martin's Lane in 1646 and was buried in St Martin's Church. He was discovered by Van Dyck and recommended to King Charles I who eventually called him 'the English Tintoret'. He was noted for his ready wit and pleasing conversation. But his rash extravagance led him into debt and penury.

The banking firm of Middleton and Campbell, forerunners of Coutts, was established here in 1692 by George Middleton, a goldsmith, and John Campbell, a relative of the Duke of Argyll. Thomas Coutts himself lived in St Martin's Lane on his marriage to his first wife. He was Scottish-born and his father had been Lord Provost of Edinburgh.

The other theatre on this side of St Martin's Lane is the New Theatre (now the Albery; see page 162). I shall ever have a particular fondness for the New Theatre, as I first entered it on the evening of my first day in London (on a day trip from Glasgow). There and then I saw a favourite actor, Henry Ainley, playing Benedick to the Beatrice of Madge Titheradge. That was early in 1926, and I should hesitate to confess how lofty was my seat or how distant my view of that *Much Ado About Nothing*. This theatre first opened in 1903 with a revival of the sweet-and-silly old play called *Rosemary*, in which played Charles Wyndham (who built and owned the house) and his wife Mary Moore, whose gaiety and charm still echo down the ages as being those of an absolutely first-rate comédienne. In its very first year Forbes Robertson and Mrs Patrick Campbell also played at the New Theatre in various plays. Thither in 1904 came Cyril Maude, and Julia Neilson and Fred Terry, the latter couple giving there their very first performance of *The Scarlet Pimpernel*, which saw the light on 5th January 1905, exactly two days before I first saw it myself.

It was at the New Theatre in 1919 that Katharine Cornell, the superb American actress, made her only appearance in London, the part being Jo in *Little Women*; and it was there in the following year that Noël Coward made his London debut as a playwright with the light comedy *I'll Leave It To You*.

The New was associated for many years with the dignified name of Matheson Lang, and it was here in 1924 that was staged the first production of Shaw's *Saint Joan* with the unsurpassed Sybil Thorndike at the head of a glowing company. I was lucky enough to see this as a student at Glasgow on its provincial tour at the end of the run. The remarkable cast was as in London, except that Harold Scott took over the Dauphin from Ernest Thesiger.

At the New, when I came to live in London, was running *The Constant Nymph* which I saw on the occasion of a new young actor called John Gielgud taking over the part of Lewis Dodd from Noël Coward. I remember thinking, even then, that the new young actor would look more at ease in costume than in modern dress and black-rimmed spectacles. At this same theatre, later, he was to play Richard of Bordeaux, Hamlet, André Obey's Noah, and more Shakespeare, and some unforgettable Chekov. Here, furthermore, in 1944 came the Old Vic Theatre Company, bombed out from Waterloo, and we there beheld great things like Ralph Richardson's Falstaff and Cyrano, and Laurence Olivier's Oedipus and Shallow and Hotspur and King Lear. They did not return to their rebuilt South Bank home until 1950. To the New Theatre one night in 1944 I escorted the ravishing Vivien Leigh to a revival of *Arms and the Man*, on which occasion I wore—as I had to—the uniform of a R.N. Sick Berth Attendant. And never shall I forget the astounded and even indignant expression of a high-ranking naval officer whose feet we had to cross to get into our seats. It was almost as good as the play.

There is one other theatre in St Martin's Lane, and this is on the other side of the narrow street, the side that more strictly belongs to the province of this book. This is the vast Coliseum, which has become the permanent new home of the Sadler's Wells Opera Company. This theatre, first opened in 1904, was a major musical hall and was still so when I first settled in London in 1926. To build it Oswald Stoll purchased a number of mainly ramshackle tenements at the southern end of the street or very near it. The area purchased was bounded by May's Buildings and Brydges Place with Bedfordbury at the rear. It was a grandiose theatre, even bigger than Drury Lane which was till then the biggest in London. It housed spectacle and ballet; musical comedy, American, British and Continental; drama and melodrama; even the circus. But it was primarily and lastingly a variety-house, the great home of the music-hall. The huge front-curtain, painted by Byam Shaw, showed every kind of variety artist who had appeared here, as well as many a singing and acting and dancing star. This curtain disgracefully vanished and fell to pieces in the end. It was finally painted over when the canvas was cracked beyond repair and it is said to have been cut up around the year 1956 to provide covers for rostrums. The historian of the Coliseum, the dramatic critic Felix Barker, was unable to find any reproduction of this famous curtain with which to grace his conscientious book.

A memorable date in the history of the Coliseum was the last performance of one of its supreme stars, Vesta Tilley, who left the stage in order to take over her private role as Lady de Frece. Mr Barker has worthily described that great and saddening occasion:

'Never in the history of the variety stage have there been scenes to equal Vesta Tilley's final call. There were seventeen curtains. There were so many flowers that the stage became a bower of them. There was Ellen Terry to come on the stage and make a graceful speech. And then came the greatest surprise of all—Vesta Tilley was presented with a set of books containing signatures which had been collected from two million of her admirers all over the country.

'Fighting back tears the small figure in khaki with the short, masculine hair-cut stood in the centre of the great stage and tried to remember all her carefully prepared phrases about kind hearts being more than coronets. She managed a few sentences, and then the whole occasion overwhelmed her as she broke down. Quickly Ellen Terry stepped forward and clasped her in her arms. The curtains came down for the last time. The audience crowded out into the London night. They remembered Ellen Terry's allusion to the war now two years over—"She made us laugh, when God knows we needed to laugh." They had seen that evening the last of a variety star who belonged to an already legendary period of the past.'

In 1968 the Coliseum became the central London home of the Sadler's Wells opera. Among its first productions was Berlioz's *Damnation of Faust* in good time for the hundredth anniversary of the death in 1869 of the great French composer.

Opposite the New Theatre is little New Row, formerly New Street. It runs gently upwards from St Martin's Lane to Garrick Street, to be continued in King Street, Covent Garden. This neat little street was 'new' in the year 1644, when it was built by the first Duke of Bedford on the site of Castle and Sunne Alley. No houses of that date survive. From the start most of its shops appear to have belonged to small traders, and it is still inclined to be a street of small trades—coffee shops (for buying as well as drinking coffee), a Welsh dairy, a stationer, two bakers (in my time), the 'Theatre Zoo' and taverns at either end. In the late seventeenth century New Street had one stately house, at the east end of the south side, on the site of the present No. 14, and we know that this was occupied from 1677 by the Countess of Chesterfield who was loved by, and also painted by, Sir Anthony Van Dyck, the court painter of whom it was said that 'his life matched in luxury that of his clients'. Historical surveyors tend to be fearful snobs and can verify and perpetuate such details about 'the quality' and yet be not nearly so conscientious about intellect and oddity in humankind. No one, for example, has noted where in New Street was the plaster-cast shop 'at the sign of the Golden Head' kept by John Flaxman, Blake's friend; or where was the eating-house frequented by Dr Johnson when, on his first coming to London, he was lodging at the house of a Mr Norris in Exeter Street across the Market. Johnson once said to Boswell: 'I dined very well for eightpence, with very good company at the Pine Apple in New Street just by where several of them (its frequenters) had travelled; they expected to meet every day, but did not know one another's names. It used to cost the rest a shilling, for they drank wine; but I had a cut of meat for sixpence, and bread for a penny, and gave the waiter a penny; so that I was quite well served, nay, better than the rest, for they gave the waiter nothing.'

The actress-novelist Mrs Inchbald, who was living in Russell Street, Covent Garden (in a building that was formerly Button's Coffee House), is said to have gone frolicsome one evening and rung all the bells in New Street and King Street without waiting. This confession was imparted to her diary. But since she unfortunately destroyed the diary on the advice of a confessor in the convent home for the aged where she died, it would not be exactly easy to prove the authenticity of this madcap tale.

At the sign of the Golden Harp, somewhere in this same little street, Benjamin Cooke sold and published music, including that of Corelli, the two Scarlattis, and Charles Avison, of Newcastle. Cooke was a prolific composer himself, a pupil of Dr Pepusch, of *Beggar's Opera* fame, and he ended his career in a blaze of quiet glory as organist at St Martin-in-the-Fields a hundred yards away.

The narrow Goodwin's Court (formerly Fisher's Alley) leads to Bedfordbury on the south side of New Row. The court is a retreat of pleasant portals and a graceful bow-windowed terrace of seventeenth-century houses. This is—or was—an oasis of quietude.

By the mild tributary of New Row we are led into the comparatively modern Garrick Street, which connects Bedford Street with Cranbourn Street. Immeasurably the most important and imposing building is the Garrick Club, which has been here since 1864. The Club was originally founded in 1831 at 35 King Street, round the corner and only just out of sight. Here it began its noble career as one where 'actors and men of education and refinement might meet on equal terms'. Among the original members was that peerless potentate among poetasters, Samuel Rogers, whom I have always regarded— perhaps with some of the prejudice of a fundamentally 'unclubable' man—as the club bore to end club bores. Anyhow, whether my instinct be sound or unsound, Samuel Rogers was born in 1763 and died, still an eminently 'clubable' man, in 1855 when he was but ninety-two.

Altogether more exciting among the original members were Count D'Orsay (who loved Lady Blessington and disastrously married her daughter) and the Rev. R. H. Barham, who wrote once popular stories in verse form, the *Ingoldsby Legends*. But the very first fact to set down about the Garrick Club is the negative one that Garrick was *not* its founder. He died in 1779, half a century before his most lasting memorial was built. In the words of this institution's historian: 'Though the Club possesses much that was his, from his birth certificate to his dress sword, from his wig powder-puff to his fishing rod, it is only from the Elysian Fields that Garrick could ever appreciate the honour of a Club to his memory.'

Other original members, besides the three already mentioned, were playwright John Poole (who wrote at least two farces tremendously successful in their day—*Paul Pry* and *Lodgings for Single Gentlemen*); playwright J. R. Planché, a prolific writer whose work is annually used as a quarry for the punning old annual pantomime at the Players Theatre (since a punnier playwright never did exist); the musician Sir George Smart, who visited Beethoven in Vienna and died at ninety; James Smith, author with his brother Horace of *Rejected Addresses*, parodies in verse which still crackle with wit; and two famous publishers in John Murray and Richard Bentley. Among the actors who were original members were Charles Kemble and W. C. Macready, Charles Mathews and his son, Charles James Mathews; and among the nobility or 'the ranks of the aristocracy', a duke, five marquesses, six earls and twelve barons.

Also of unquestionable dignity among the first members were Serjeant (later Mr Justice) Talfourd, who wrote frigid tragedies for Macready, and John Lockhart, who wrote a fine life of Scott and a less fine life of Burns. But the dignity of some of the other early members was slightly more in question: George Wombwell, for instance, who founded the menagerie with a non-member called Bostock; and Alfred Bunn, a flagrantly bad poet and a muddling manager for a time of both Drury Lane and Covent Garden. Of the latter member the Club's historian has written: 'Bunn's poetic soul had been driven frantic by the tastelessness of the public, the aloofness of authors, the conceit of adapters, the oppression of the censor, and the scurrility of the Press—above all by the vanity and contentiousness of actors.'

Even more perceptively it was said of Thackeray, who was an early member and became almost the best-loved of all: 'He was the choice spirit of the Garrick Club, who was during his time the Club itself—its centre, its soul, its cynosure. It seemed for him a sort of whetting-stone of his wit; it kept his humour bright, keen and polished; his fine, large capacities filled the place.' His great rival among novelists, Charles Dickens, was elected as member some four years after Thackeray. The rivalry was perfectly friendly until a journalist friend of Dickens, Edmund Yates, wrote an article on Thackeray which gave its subject great offence. The so-called Garrick Club Affair of 1858 was the result, and it set up a long-lasting coldness between the two great novelists. Years and years passed, during which the two men ignored each other even when in the same room. Then there came a day, early in December 1863, when they met face to face in another London club, The Athenaeum. They were about to pass each other in the hall when both hesitated, and they spontaneously shook hands and exchanged smiles and then friendly words. Within a fortnight of this reunion Thackeray had died and Dickens went to his funeral on 30th December.

Six months later the stately new premises of the Garrick Club opened, on 4th July 1864. The new street had been named Garrick Street on the representation of the Club. It replaced a formerly congested area of alleys between King Street, Floral Street and St Martin's Lane.

It is not my intention to give here anything more than a personal and therefore biased sketch of the Garrick Club's great collection of theatre pictures. The basis of the collection was a series of scenes and portraits amassed by Charles Mathews, the Elder, a masterly comedian and a mimic of genius (1776–1835). This core of a collection was presented to the Club, in its first home in King Street, by John Rowland Durrant. Later came 116 water-colours from the great comedian's son, Charles James Mathews (a nimble actor likewise, who married Mme Vestris). Bequests since then have been abundant, and they may be said to have reached their culmination in some (again mainly theatrical) pictures from the collections of various actor-members. The picture which interests me as much as any other (and which I never visit the Club without gazing upon for a rapt minute or two) is that of the closing scene in Massinger's *A New Way to Pay Old Debts*, which rightly has pride of place on the main staircase. The painter of this marvellously dramatic picture (Pl. 34) was George Clint (1770–1854). Born in Drury Lane and, like Turner, the son of a hairdresser, he was first apprenticed to a fishmonger. Not only does his masterpiece show Edmund Kean at the height of his powers and intensely alive at the stage's dead centre; it also shows Clint himself standing modestly and in stage-costume (second from the left) among the rest of the company. Kean's facial resemblance here to Laurence Olivier seems to me marked and startling. This is only one out of fifteen pictures by George Clint in the Garrick Club. It formerly hung in the Beefsteak Room of the Lyceum Theatre till one day when Henry Irving himself is reported to have said: 'The Garrick Club is the right place for that picture. Here it is hidden away—there it will be seen by many.' So there it went.

Nearly all of the English painters who have relished painting actors in action—from Lawrence to Sickert, from Zoffany to Nicholson and Pryde—are finely represented in the Garrick Club. There are no fewer than 170 small theatrical portraits by Samuel de Wilde, who seems never to have painted any other sort of picture. There are portraits by Forbes-Robertson, who was quite as happy at the easel as on the stage. There are even portraits of present-day actors and dramatists, or at least of such as have recently died.

There are also several portraits of Master Henry West Betty—including full-length and life-size—upon which I never gaze without having my belief confirmed that here was a considerable actor as well as a beautiful and exceedingly well-graced infant. You have only to make this observation—in the Club or elsewhere—to have the sight of heterosexual eyebrows shooting up into embarrassed brows! The Young Roscius, as they called him, was a Shropshire lad, born at Shrewsbury in 1791. He became an actor at the age of eleven, and had conquered Belfast and the English provinces before he was fifteen. He then marched on to London and conquered that likewise. He *took* the Country and then the Town in parts like Hamlet, Richard III and the title-part in John Home's *Douglas*. To anyone not blinded by prejudiced blinkers he was and remains a very beautiful youth. But he had a beauteous voice also—until it broke, as voices will. The pleasing pipe turned one day into a gruff and quite unmusical instrument. And Master Betty's stage-career was over at sixteen, though he had still fifty years to live—and a well-earned fortune to live on—after his final retirement in 1824. He died on 24th August 1874—on the very day that another precocious long-liver, Max Beerbohm, became two years old.

At one time I planned a little book founded on this accidental link, which I intended to call *Max and Master Betty*. But I am a writer easily forestalled, and quite recently Mr Giles Playfair, that redoubtable authority on Edmund Kean, duly forestalled me by giving the world a little book on Master Betty himself which leaves the likes of me nothing whatever to say. This appeared in 1967 and is entitled *The Prodigy: the Strange Life of Master Betty*. Mr Playfair quotes the bad critics as well as the good ones, and the gush of duchesses and of politicians; moreover he strongly implies that William Hough, the boy's first acting tutor, was a scallywag and a sod. He also quotes the foolish fashionable press of the day: 'Female beauty cannot afford anything more sweet than his smile,' said *The Lady's Monthly Museum* of January 1805. 'The whole town is in love with him,' *The Morning Post* declared on 8th March 1805, 'even if he can't feel love.' Professor John Robison compared him with an 'unprotected Beauty'; and, unprotected or not, Master Betty appears to have had, for high and low alike, something rather more than the glamour of a female film star in our own time.

But to my relief and delight Mr Playfair restores the balance by repeating the fair opinion of William Hazlitt, who was in all senses the fairest and soundest of all dramatic critics. Unfortunately the Betty-mania smote the country before Hazlitt was in practice; but in his youth he saw the marvellous boy as Douglas, and wrote in his *Table-Talk* (1822): 'Master Betty's acting was a singular phenomenon, but it was also as beautiful as it was singular. I saw him in the part of Douglas, and he seemed almost like "some gay creature of the element", moving about gracefully, with all the flexibility of youth, and murmuring Æolian sounds with plaintive tenderness. . . .' Alas, the sounds became less Æolian! But Hazlitt adds a footnote telling how he once met the actor who was already retired yet only about thirty years old:

'I had the pleasure of spending an evening with Mr. Betty, when we had some "good talk" about the good old times of acting. I wanted to insinuate that I had been a sneaking admirer, but could not bring it in. As, however, we were putting on our great coats downstairs, I ventured to break the ice by saying, "There is one actor of that period of whom we have not made honourable mention, I mean Master Betty." "Oh!" he said, "I have forgot all that." I replied, that *he* might, but that I could not forget the pleasure I had in seeing him. On which he turned off, and shaking his sides heartily, and with no measured demands on his lungs, called out, "Oh, memory! memory!" in a way that showed he felt the full force of the illusion. I found afterwards that the subject did not offend, and we were to have drunk some Burton-ale together the following evening, but were prevented. I hope he will consider that the engagement still stands good.'

Thus told by Hazlitt himself, the anecdote seems to me to bring out the best of both young men, the critic and the actor.

There are also in the Garrick Club innumerable stage relics and properties of infinite fascination, as well as countless letters in careful store, of which I have asked permission to copy and reproduce only one. It is a letter from David Garrick himself to a lady of quality who had tried to win the great actor's interest in the potentialities of a young friend ambitious to go on the stage. Addressed to the Duchess of Portland and dated 29th October 1767, it was given by the present Duke of Portland to the Garrick Club through the good offices of a club member, Mr Raymond Massey:

'Madam,—I shall always be happy to obey your Grace's commands, but our Company at present is so full, and all the Parts dispos'd of, that I could not without great injustice to those Actors I have already engag'd, employ the person you recommend.

'I have given Mr Collins the best advice in my Power and

appris'd him that I shall be ready at the End of the Season to examine his qualifications for the Stage – – – if your Grace will permit me to speak my mind, I think he has the most unpromising Aspect for an Actor I ever saw, a small pair of unmeaning Eyes stuck on a round unthinking face are not the most desirable requisites for a Hero, or a fine Gentleman. However I will give him a Tryal if he is unemployed at that time of the year so if he can be of the least service to me or himself I shall most certainly obey Your Grace's Commands. Mrs Garrick presents her respects to your Grace and thinks herself greatly honour'd by your mention of her.'

The letter is just one brief and tiny example of the Club's vast treasury of papers and documents of the sort. But I have long been lost in admiration of the manner in which this particular example begins in the strain of elegant politeness, deviates with not too swift a suddenness into shrewd plain-speaking good sense, and then, to conclude, reverts into the formal manners of its century.

It would be invidious to give a list of the several publishers, actors, playwrights and colleagues in criticism who have been my occasional hosts in the Garrick Club. But I cannot forbear to mention the most veteran member in my time, Sir Bronson Albery, who has, recently and twice within a year, said to me there: 'The theatre misses such a critic as you, Jock Dent.' No words from so distinguished a source could be possibly pleasanter to my ears—and I heard them twice, with only a few months between the two occasions. And I must finally divulge that my old chief, James Agate, would dearly have liked to be enrolled as a member but was blackballed or disqualified for his pains. Thereupon he wrote a letter to the Club's Secretary (I know because I took it down myself, secretarially) which contained the sentence: 'I am not in the least surprised. A large number of your members would have blackballed David Garrick himself.' Something I have recently learned would have given old Jimmy great glee in his shades. It is the news that Henry Irving himself was blackballed from the Garrick Club some years before he was eventually elected in 1874.

CHAPTER SEVEN

THE HEART OF THE MARKET

Before leaving Southampton Street, Strand, one should perhaps have pointed out that it was there, in the temporary residence of a Miss Sally Forester, that James Boswell (Pl. 18) lost his virginity, or at least his London virginity. But let that prince of diarists tell the story in his own inimitable expository style:

'21st November, 1762. I went to Douglas's and drank tea. I next went and called in Southampton Street, for Miss Sally Forester, my first love, who lived at the Blue Periwig. I found that the people of the house were broke and dead [i.e. bankrupt and deceased] and could hear nothing of her. I also called for Miss Jeany Wells in Berwick Street, Soho, but found that she was fled, they knew not whither, and had been ruined with extravagance. Good heaven, thought I, what an amazing change in two years! I saw in the year 1760 these young ladies in all the glow of beauty and admiration; and now they are utterly erased or worse.'

Skilful editing of *The London Journal* sends us onwards, per footnotes, to later references to these lights o' love: 'Sunday, 13th March, 1763 . . . Stayed at home from church. Erskine and I took a walk to Covent Garden, and I carried him to Southampton Street and showed him the house in which I first paid my addresses to the Paphian Queen, where I first experienced the melting and transporting rites of Love.' A note declares this to have been the former lodging of Miss Sally Forester. A month later he gazes again upon the abode in company which gives him a peculiar and characteristic 'kick'. This is an instance of the essential Boswell: 'Saturday, 9th April . . . I was diverted at walking the streets of London with Dr Blair [a divine and a Professor of Rhetoric at Edinburgh]. I marched him down Southampton Street in the Strand, for the whimsical idea of passing under the windows of my first London lady of the town with an Edinburgh minister whom I had so often heard preach in the New Church. We were in good frame and talked agreeably serious.' And finally, at a circus entertainment one night in Chelsea, Boswell comes face to face again with his original charmer, who turns out to be married but not so very much the worse for hard wear:

'10th June [1763]. While I stood gazing about, whom did I suddenly perceive but—Miss Sally Forester, my first Lady of Venus's Bedchamber, whom I have sought for eagerly but could never find. I approached her with something like the air of a tragedy hero. She immediately knew me. I felt really a fine romantic sensation at meeting her. Miss Simson who lodged in the [Southampton Street] house with her and was very civil to me was with her tonight. We went into the Star and Garter, and I treated them with tea. We resumed our former adventures. I cannot express the curious feelings which I had when I looked back three years; called up my ideas then, and all that has happened to me since. Alas! my ideas have not now that giddy fervour which they had when I was first in London. However, I now walk on surer ground. She said she was married to Captain Peter Grant, a Scotch officer, and she would not allow me to renew my joy. But she promised to meet me at her companion's house, who also said she was married, and called herself Mrs Tredwell. We walked into town together. The evening was delicious, and I glowed with pleasing imagination.'

Anticipation also? We shall never know whether it was gratified, or how often. For of Miss Sally Forester or Mrs Peter Grant there is no further mention in this or the many subsequent diaries.

On 27th November of the previous year Boswell had been taken by John Beard (manager of Covent Garden Theatre and also a favourite tenor of Handel) to a meeting of the Beefsteak Club in an apartment high above the theatre. There were present other notorious celebrities and a good time was had: 'We had nothing to eat but beefsteaks, and had wine and punch in plenty and freedom. We had a number of songs.' On 20th January 1763 Boswell called on Garrick at Drury Lane Theatre and was warmly received by the great actor, who said among other things: 'Sir, you will be a very great man. And when you are so, remember the year 1763.' Boswell comments: 'What he meant by my being a great man I can understand. For really, to speak seriously, I think there is a blossom about me of something more distinguished than the generality of mankind.' He goes on to indulge in 'noble reveries' of the same sort.

But this, the most singular self-recorder who ever lived, was to remember the year 1763 for reasons unconnected with greatness and *intellectual* intercourse. On that same day, when he received Garrick's goodwill and high compliments, Boswell had had a final meeting with his courtesan, Louisa, who had infected him with a sordid (and, in those days, not easily curable) distemper. He writes: 'Thus ended my intrigue with the fair Louisa ... from which I expected at least a winter's safe copulation.' His last word on this well-loved one: 'She is in all probability a most consummate dissembling whore.'

On the self-same page and on the same day he is taking David Garrick cordially by the hand and returning his compliments with interest: 'Thou greatest of men, I cannot express how happy you make me.' And he concludes: 'This, upon my soul, was no flattery. He saw it was not. The scene gave me a charming flutter of spirits and dispelled my formal gloom.' Note that Boswell at this time was but twenty-two or twenty-three.

London did not know him well again till 1772, after his sojourn in Holland and his subsequent marriage to a Scottish gentlewoman. But in this latter year he is back again in the month of March: 'As I walked up the Strand and passed through a variety of fine girls genteely dressed, all wearing Venus's girdle [no footnote explaining this] and all inviting me to amorous intercourse, I confess I was a good deal uneasy. . . . I resolved never again to come to London without bringing my wife along with me.'

In the last few pages of a recent diary volume published in England—*The Ominous Years, 1774-1776*—we get a teasing glimpse of Boswell yet again on the chase in Covent Garden. Not by any means for the first time he seems even more interested in his own behaviour than in the lady's possibilities:

'Saturday, 13th April [1776]—Walked through Covent Garden between two and three in my way to dinner at Tom Davies's. Saw a very fine woman, elegantly dressed, moving along by herself. I passed her, but as everybody looked at her with the appearance of admiration, I could not resist stopping till she came up, and at once begged to know where she lived. She told me in Greek Street,

Soho, and her name was upon the door—Mrs Price. I walked in the Piazza with her, and was easy and gay and complimentative, and fancied I was agreeable. I trusted that nobody knew me, but Dr Johnson had counselled me not to trust too much to that.'

It is sad to learn, in passing, that the public demand in England for more of Boswell's self-revelations and self-discoveries has dropped considerably because he showed himself capable of cruelty to a dog which, by way of punishment, he allowed to run tied to his carriage for miles on end during his trip to France to see Voltaire and Rousseau. And there are still nearly twenty years of diary—he died in 1795—to be edited and published by Yale University. It may, of course, appear in America. Even so, it may be said that we know already James Boswell better than we know any other man who ever put pen to paper.

Another loose-liver and self-recorder who could not resist the temptation, in his youth at least, to wander hopefully in this beguiling and adventuresome quarter of London, was William Hickey. His name was adopted some thirty years ago by a successful London journalist for the head of his news-and-hearsay column; it is still so used, with the result that the original William Hickey is overlooked and forgotten. Yet the four volumes of his memoirs are worth seeking out. These memoirs have a history almost as extraordinary as that of Boswell's diaries. They were not written for publication, but only for the interest of Hickey's relatives and friends. He was a near-contemporary of Boswell, being born just nine years later (1749) and surviving him by twenty years or so. The two men never met, though they might easily have done so in any Covent Garden bagnio. William Hickey began his amorous operations as a schoolboy of twelve, though he was the son of Joseph Hickey, an attorney of considerable probity, eminence and wealth. He had already been seduced by his mother's companion-maid, Nancy Harris, who was dismissed on his account. In the winter of the same year Master Hickey was given a guinea by a friend of his father whom he happened to meet in the Park. The consequence is related with characteristic gusto and frankness:

'Having just then discovered the residence of my wanton little bed-fellow, Nanny Harris, I directly went to her lodgings which were in a court that ran out of Bow Street, Covent Garden. I told her the strength of my purse, and proposed going to the play, which she consenting to, there was I a hopeful sprig of 13, stuck up in a green box, with a disreputable woman. From the theatre she took me home to supper, giving me lobster and oysters, both of which she knew I was very fond of, and plenty of rum punch; with my head full of which, at a late hour I went home, and as I could not tell where I had been, I received a smart flogging from the arm of my old operator, Doctor Lloyd [his schoolmaster].'

In 1768 he has a regretful note on the passing of this regular-irregular partner of his boyhood and young manhood when 'she died, a martyr to a life of excess'.

Hickey, unlike Boswell, did occasionally try to resist temptation. He appears to have been much more addicted to gambling than was the Scotsman, and for this reason he avoided for a time going to Old Slaughter's Club, of which he had been a regular frequenter. But there came an evening when he returned and succumbed, and went deeper and deeper into vice in a way which must shock every generation (excepting the present one, which appears to be both unshockable and undisgustable) :

'In consequence of the good resolutions I made upon receiving the undeserved five guineas from my father, more than two months had elapsed without my once going to any of my old haunts, and I had during that period conducted myself with the utmost propriety and decorum. . . . My vanity even carried me so far as to suppose I now possessed fortitude sufficient to resist temptation, and that I might venture occasionally to visit the Club of Slaughters without renewing my former vicious habits. Full of this erroneous idea I, one evening in March, called in at Slaughters, where some of my quondam associates immediately gathered round me, with warm congratulations upon my return to them, protesting that they would have a gala night to celebrate the restoration of so worthy a member. Up I went to the Club room, down went the wine and punch, and away went all my plans of reformation.'

The wild young men informed Hickey that they had recently discovered 'two new houses of infinite merit', to both of which he was to be introduced that very evening. After doing 'the old Bow Street rounds' the party proceeded to a kind of den called Wetherby's 'situate in the narrowest part of Little Russell Street, Drury Lane'. At the door they were scrutinized by 'a cut-throat looking rascal' peering through a small wicket, who then admitted them one by one. This struck Hickey as like being admitted to a prison of the most horrible kind. The first spectacle they were offered was that of two half-naked, bleeding and wholly drunken women having a wrestling match: 'For several minutes not a creature interfered between them, or seemed to care a straw what mischief they might do each other, and the contest went on with unabated fury.'

Hickey was relieved when his party appeared to have had enough and decided to move to another corner of the same big room. But here a no less astonishing sight met his gaze. For here an 'uncommonly athletic young man of about twenty-five' was apparently being attacked by everybody at once: 'No less than three Amazonian tigresses were pummelling him with all their might' while the male onlookers attacked him with sticks. The central figure retaliated to the best of his considerable ability, knocking each assailant down with his fists whenever opportunity offered and whether it was a woman or a man. Hickey unavailingly tried to slip away from it all, but he was angrily seized upon by the Cerberus at the outer door who said: 'What! Do you want to tip us a bilk? Have you paid your reckoning, eh? No, no, youngster, no tricks upon travellers. No exit here until you have passed muster, my chick!'

Hickey writes: 'In this dreadful hole I was therefore obliged to stay until my friends chose to depart.' In the street he expressed his disgust to his companions. But they laughed heartily at his innocence, and they had singularly little difficulty in persuading him not to run off to home and safety but instead to join them in a visit to the second of their new haunts, called Murphy's (which at the end of that same year changed its name to Marjoram's). This 'scene of nocturnal dissoluteness' was in the same street as Wetherby's but on the opposite side. It also served strong drink until five in the morning, whereas Wetherby's summarily stopped supplies at three. It seems to have extended its licence in other respects also.

If the happenings at Wetherby's were unspeakable, those at Murphy's or Marjoram's would seem to have been unwriteable, for Hickey does not even attempt to describe them. He says only: 'From this latter nest of pickpockets, and lowest description of prostitutes, we got away about half-past four, I inwardly wishing every mishap might attend me if ever I again crossed the threshold of either of the Russell Street houses during the remainder of my life.'

That was in March, and Master Hickey was back again at both resorts in May making the acquaintance of 'temporary hostesses' with names like Mother Hamilton and Mother Cocksedge. At Wetherby's he found the two violent lady wrestlers to be the best of friends—a Miss Burgess who sang very well and a 'sad profligate girl' who had justly acquired the name of Blasted Bet Wilkinson. Hickey communicates a nice bit of gossip about Charles Dibdin: 'This Miss Burgess lived for several years afterwards with Dibdin, the actor, who had just at the above period commenced his theatrical career in the character of Hodge in the comic opera of *The Maid of the Mill*.' The other previous happening at Wetherby's was now explained to Hickey, and he duly explains it in his turn: 'The other battle royal arose from the man (who was a notorious woman's bully) having basely robbed the two who attacked him, that the rest concerned were the friends of one party or the other, and acted accordingly.' Whether the phrase in parenthesis means 'the bully of a notorious woman' or whether a 'woman's bully' was a cant phrase for a pimp, or a stallion, or some such calling are questions which one must leave to the nice taste and judgment of the gentle reader.

At Murphy's on this return visit William Hickey happened upon another subject for scandalous and well-founded gossip. He found the place 'well stowed, a large crowd being collected round the famous and popular Ned Shuter who, although immoderately drunk, was entertaining the circle of bystanders with all sorts of buffoonery and tricks'. Seats were readily placed for the newcomers, and for more than an hour the celebrated actor 'kept us in a continued roar of laughter when he suddenly fell from his seat as if he had been shot, and I really feared he was dead, until those better acquainted than myself observed if he was it was only dead drunk, a finale nightly repeated'. Shuter was then lifted up and carried 'like a hog' to his lodgings in the immediate neighbourhood. Here Hickey has the final comment: 'We departed to our beds, I being as much pleased with the night's amusement as I had on the former been disgusted.' Edward Shuter, a great comedian with an extraordinarily malleable face, and seen here in his cups at the age of forty, was later to become the first Old Hardcastle (Goldsmith) and Sir Anthony Absolute (Sheridan).

In the winter of 1771 Hickey made the acquaintance of a quartet of wild young sparks who were the original 'Mohawks', so called after a particularly savage Red Indian tribe. The first quartet to earn and deserve this name, which the dictionary defines as a class of aristocratic ruffians who infested the streets by night in the eighteenth century, were Rhoan Hamilton, later to be known as the Irish Rebel who called himself Hamilton Rhoan; Mr Hayter, whose father was a wealthy merchant and bank director; Mr Osborne, a young American who had come here to study law and studied lawlessness instead; and Mr Frederick, a handsome lad without a guinea but said to be a son, or possibly a grandson, of the unfortunate Theodore, King of Corsica. These four, by the profligacy of their manners and their outrageous conduct in the theatres, taverns and coffee houses in the vicinity of Covent Garden, created general indignation and alarm, actually (says Hickey) 'driving away many sedate persons from their customary amusement in an evening'.

Hickey, according to himself, and not without some hint of cant, deplored the disgraceful manners of this quartet and avoided quarrelling with them. Early in 1774 they were at long last seized by the police. Hamilton decamped to France, first paying most of his debts; Hayter was sent by his father to Holland; and Osborne, bankrupt and disgraced, returned to America, taking with him his young friend Frederick, who joined the English troops there and was dead in action in a twelvemonth. Hickey was left to moralize: 'Thus ended the career of four young men who, for a period of three years, continued in one uninterrupted course of folly, intemperance and riot, to the utter disgrace of themselves and of the police of the capital, which was either so relaxed or so corrupt as to permit their course of iniquity to proceed uninterrupted.' Such were the original 'Mohawks'.

In the second volume of his diary Hickey tells us how he was sent to India to take up a post there. He returned on leave in 1774 and has little to report on the state of Covent Garden, which, of course, he revisited. His third volume is wholly devoted to his existence in Bengal in which, at last, he reaches years of discretion. He never, or hardly ever, descends into dullness, but he does ascend into propriety, which means a lesser degree of readability. In the fourth and final volume he had retired and settled down to grow old in Beaconsfield, where still lived his father's old client, the mellow great man called Edmund Burke. The latter died in November 1797, and Hickey—himself approaching fifty by this time—wrote nobly about him. Hickey lived on to be seventy, or some say even eighty, spending his last years in Little Hall Barn, a charming old house at the Windsor end of the village. The recent discovery of this fact gives me a peculiar pleasure since I have inhabited the same desultory town for twelve years and hope to go on living there to the age of seventy—or even eighty or ninety. Little Hall Barn was, before Hickey bought it, the residence of one Edmund Waller, a direct descendant of the Cavalier poet remembered for 'Go, Lovely Rose', who lies in the nearby churchyard under a very old walnut tree. Little Hall Barn was the residence of Lord Burnham before he moved to the adjacent and aloof Hall Barn itself. In answer to a letter of enquiry the present Lord Burnham confirms my impression that Henry Irving was a quite frequent guest at Hall Barn in the late 'nineties, and that Ellen Terry quite often came as well.

A final odd fact about William Hickey is that his autobiography remained unpublished until the present century. The first volume appeared and made a great stir in 1913. Said *The Daily News*: 'One of the happiest discoveries of recent years, Hickey's autobiography has been compared to Smollett and indeed in its breeziness and variety it deserves the comparison.'

We now reach the last stage of our circumambulation of Covent Garden—the church of St Paul and its churchyard-cum-garden—bounded on the south by Henrietta Street, on the west by the middle section of Bedford Street, and on the north by King Street (in the centre of which I lived in a top-floor flat from the middle thirties to the middle forties).

It is a rectangle round which one can walk unhurriedly—hurry is here impossible, for a dozen reasons—in less than five minutes; and one can begin, just as one can end, on the east side of the rectangle which has the old church's original blind portico facing, and indeed part of, the Piazza or Main Market from which we set out on our survey.

Henrietta Street, like King Street, is no more than 150 yards long. But only King Street and Bedford Street excel it in the Marlovian quality of possessing 'infinite riches in a little room'. Its associations are principally artistic, literary and theatrical. It was built around the year 1637.

One of its first residents was a brilliant miniaturist, Samuel Cooper, who made striking likenesses of Arlington and Ashley (both of the 'Cabal'); also of the Duchess of Richmond 'before her having the small-pox, and it would make a man weep to see what she was then, and what she is like to be, by people's discourse, now'. Pepys himself visited Cooper here more than once, and commissioned a portrait of Mrs Pepys. On one of his visits he particularly admired Cromwell's famous picture with the warts all complete. Pepys had a few doubts about Cooper's skill as a painter, but found him in most other respects a man after his own heart: 'Now I understand his great skill in musick, his playing and setting to the French lute most excellently, and he speaks French, and indeed is an excellent man.'

Another painter who came to reside in this street in the eighteenth century was Samuel Scott, who has been nicknamed 'the English Canaletto'. In his house he formed a club—a non-social club—of only six members, and they included a very odd and remarkable man-of-all-the-arts called Marcellus Laroon, in whom nowadays there is a considerable revival of interest. He was the son of another painter of the same name, a man of Dutch-French descent, who was living in Bow Street in 1680, not far from Will's Coffee House. He was employed by Sir Godfrey Kneller as an assistant. He had a passion for music as well as painting, and passed this on to his two sons, John and Marcellus. The latter lived to be ninety-three in 1772. The Laroons deserve a little book all to themselves, and indeed there is a treasurable brochure by Mr Basil Taylor, who prepared it for the Paul Mellon Foundation in 1967. Watteau was the great influence on the Laroons, and their exquisite and charming rococo art proves it was a healthy influence.

The Society of Arts—not yet Royal—founded itself in Henrietta Street in 1754, at Rawthmell's Coffee House whose exact site is now doubtful. Some twenty years later this distinguished Society, after meeting in various places, settled in what are to this day its handsome quarters in The Adelphi, built by the Adam brothers. Long before this —in the year 1762—its members numbered over 2,500, and among the signatures in the first subscription book are those of Horace Walpole, Thomas Chippendale, Joshua Reynolds, Samuel Richardson, Edward Gibbon, Robert Adam, William Hogarth and Samuel Johnson. On one occasion Johnson told Boswell that the members at the Society's meetings were such a distinguished gathering that when he tried to speak at a meeting 'all his flowers of oratory forsook him'. Not until the present writer was invited to lecture to the Royal Society of Arts (in 1969, a year in which he was already engaged on this history), and did so in the form of a paper entitled 'The Fine Art of Criticism'—not till then did he realize that he possessed no flowers of oratory whatsoever, and that those he previously had imagined in his possession had already withered in the bud before he reached the age of sixty. But that is by the way, and not wholly serious!

It was in Henrietta Street that at one time dwelt Kitty Clive, who lived from 1711 till 1785, who acted often with Garrick, and was a favourite of playgoers as dissimilar as Horace Walpole and Dr Johnson. It has been said of Mrs Clive that 'though not strictly beautiful she was so charming and animated that she achieved a great reputation in the playing of high-spirited comedy'. Also that 'she first charmed the audience by her singing'. The same things have been said much nearer our own time about Dame Marie Tempest, who died in 1942 at the age of seventy-eight.

Another one-time resident of Henrietta Street was the Irish-born dramatist Thomas Southerne, who wrote *The Fatal Marriage* and thus provided the great part of Isabella for Mrs Woffington in 1755 and for Mrs Siddons in 1782—in fact, a play which stayed popular for nearly a century. Southerne, a noted and respected figure in Covent Garden, often attended evening prayers at St Paul's Church, 'always neat and decently dressed, commonly in black, with his silver sword and silver locks'. He spent his later years in Westminster, but when he died he returned home and was buried in St Paul's Church, Covent Garden.

Hannah More, the bluestocking who wrote pious verses and who comforted Mrs Garrick when she lost her great husband, also lived here when in London. And it was in Henrietta Street that Jane Austen came to stay for several weeks with her brother, who worked in a bank nearby. It was from No. 10, in 1813, that Miss Austen wrote a few of those plain and prim and homely letters that are so unsparkling in comparison with her novels. The actress Frances Maria Kelly was residing at No. 8 in 1819, when Charles Lamb (then at Nos. 20–21 Russell Street) proposed marriage to her. He was rejected by return of post, 'frankly and decidedly', in her own words. Lamb answered the rejection with a much shorter note beginning: 'Your injunctions shall be obeyed to a tittle.' Hazlitt said of Miss Kelly's Lucy Lockit that she was 'a charming little vixen' with 'the most agreeable pout in the world and the best-humoured smile'.

At the end of the eighteenth century Paul Whitehead lived in

Henrietta Street—one of the rakes of the Hell Fire Club which used to go devil-worshipping at Medmenham and West Wycombe in Bucks. Neither a tremendous poet nor a tremendous rake, Whitehead nevertheless had his epitaph written by David Garrick himself. In 1893 Charles Frohman, the American impresario, opened his first London office here, at No. 4. He has already been dealt with in my comments on the Duke of York's Theatre, but he was perhaps the best-known American theatre-manager throughout his long career which terminated with the sinking of the *Lusitania* in May 1915. It can have been only a few weeks earlier that in Glasgow I was taken to see a jolly revue called *The Passing Show of 1915*. The Showman's song at the start— sung by a big breezy American comedian called Fred Duprez—found a rhyme for 'I'm the showman—the cheery beery Showman' in words 'like Mr Charley Frohman'! Of course, I asked my elders who this could be and was promptly told. The news of the great manager's dramatic death around the same time must have fixed this rhyme in my memory for good. The show also contained one of my heart's many delights, Miss Ella Retford. (For anyone who cares, the book of the revue was by Arthur Wimperis and the music by Herman Finck.)

In a high attic near the south-west corner of Henrietta Street there has long lived—and still blessedly lives—a dear little old maid called 'Liddy' who was my twice-a-week charwoman from 1938 till 1943, when I lived in King Street (Pls. 36, 37). Early in the wartime blackout, in 1940, she was knocked down by a market lorry. She told me all about it afterwards, when she had made a complete and miraculous recovery. She is, and always was, bright, cheerful, dauntless—and tiny—no taller than a London parking meter. She is also, and always was, proudly and triumphantly Cockney, and just as much 'pure Dickens' as Charles Laughton's Drury Lane landlady can have been. She was born and bred in Covent Garden. When the accident happened on a winter evening in 1940 she was immediately rushed to hospital and, apparently, given every intimation that she had not much hope of recovery (for she admitted then and there to being nearly seventy). There was to be a major operation. But before that happened there arrived in the ward a parson and three choirboys to read to her and sing to her for the comfort of her soul. 'But I ain't a-goin' to die' protested my little charlady. Nevertheless, the parson read a chapter or a prayer and the choirboys sang *Nearer my God to Thee*, which my old Liddy did not like at all, calling it in her subsequent narration to me 'an 'orrid old 'ymn any'ow'. Then the anaesthetist arrived, and almost the next thing Liddy knew (after a vague recollection of seeing the surgical instruments which she described as 'a lot of knives and forks laid out on a table') was the gradual return to her senses, to behold a man in white bending over her. 'Did you speak to him?' I asked as she paused. 'Yes, indeed I did,' replied Liddy, laughing at the recollection. 'I did such a silly thing. I said to him, "Are you Jesus?"' It is clear and very touching that my old Liddy thought in the middle of her ordeal that she had entered Heaven, in spite of her determination not to go there yet awhile. She told me, after her operation, that she had never felt better in her life. She had been safe in the arms of—the surgeon.

This true little account—absolutely unaltered and unelaborated—I wrote in *The Strand Magazine* early in 1943, when the magazine had been reduced to pocket-size and was within a few years of vanishing for good in 1950. The anecdote served me well as a peg for an article whose aim was to persuade readers not to be scared of the surgeon's knife; and to it the editor—now my old friend, Reginald Pound—had given the good comprehensive title: 'Afraid Of The Surgeon's Knife? Most People Are: But There Is No Reason Why They Should Be.' The peg of the essay could hardly have been more efficacious or more Covent-Gardenish.

The north side of Henrietta Street has its middle taken up by the façade of St Peter's Hospital, which has always concentrated on kidney and kindred troubles. To its west is something describing itself as the Metropolitan Regional Examination Board; this occupies the site of Offley's, a tavern frequented by Charles Dickens and famous for its chops and its ales. Here also is a fine Italianate building painted creamy white with a bright Della Robbia blue on its eyelids so to speak, i.e. the spaces above its windows. This handsome building at the corner of Bedford Street, originally Woburn Chambers, is called today Alginate House because it is the office of a firm which extracts commercial products from seaweeds or *algae*. To the east of the hospital are some solicitors, a café and a bank, and the little shop of a stationer, Mr Macnamara, so courteous and obliging that Clemence Dane mentioned his amiability in her book, *London Has A Garden*, and so therefore do I in mine.

The gateway into St Paul's churchyard and church is Inigo Place, which contains a house occupied for many years by the actor Ben

Webster and his actress-wife Dame May Whitty. Both loved and revered Ellen Terry, and so both have tablets to their memory inside the church and near the silver urn containing the ashes of the still adored old Ellen herself. Immediately north of the gateway we are at No. 29–30, a goodish building which has seen more imposing days (Pl. 39), though its three eleven-windowed upper storeys still have their effect. The building is now occupied by a chartered architect, but before 1969 had always been a publisher's premises. More than seventy years ago it was the headquarters of Messrs Macmillan. For what happened in 1897 let me quote the words of the late J. M. Dent in his memoirs:

'Towards the end of this year—1897—Messrs Macmillan completed their new building in St. Martin's Street [it was demolished in 1969], and their old premises—29–30 Bedford Street—were to let. There was a remainder of fifteen years of the lease to run and the rent was £750 a year, with all the repairs! and it staggered us at first. Still it was a great temptation to take over the house with which so many of the great names of the century had been associated —Maurice, Kingsley, Tom Hughes, Huxley, Tyndall, Tennyson and many another. We decided to burn our ships and take it, though we had to rely upon subletting a considerable portion. The venture proved quite successful as our business at once increased and continued to do so uninterruptedly for many years.'

The removal to the new site at the corner of Bedford Street and Chandos Place and the raising of the new building, Aldine House, are only sketched by the founder of this firm. But what he does permit himself to write is eminently readable:

'It was good to be able to have our premises built as we desired them, and I had great fun and interest in getting the architect, Mr Purchase, to give me what I wanted, and at last I was quite satisfied with his plans, though the cost of putting up such a building was enormous. Again this called for more capital, which we had to set to work to earn, yet we could not see any other way out if we were to carry on Everyman's Library. ... The building is a great pleasure to me. I had my own way with the façade—a blend of Elizabethan and Queen Anne styles—and I cannot help feeling that it is at once modest and dignified. ... We opened the premises in November 1911.'

Five years before this, in 1906, the first fifty titles of Everyman's Library were published simultaneously. They cost one shilling a volume. Between then and 1911, when Aldine House was built and opened, 500 titles of this marvellous series of inexpensive classics had appeared in the Edwardian world.

My father had purchased a few of them, including Boswell's *Life of Samuel Johnson*, which were Nos. 1 and 2 on the list. These two and Pepys's Diary, which was contained in Nos. 53 and 54, and therefore must have been in the second batch of titles, were the first four volumes in my father's bookcase, which also contained, as I clearly remember and as the years went on, Everyman volumes of Dickens, Herrick, Tolstoy, Balzac, Hazlitt, Ruskin, Dumas, Ibsen, Hakluyt (though only one of no fewer than eight somewhat oddly devoted to that Tudor geographer), and Captain Marryat's *The Settlers in Canada*, the last given to me on my eleventh birthday.

Ideally I should keep myself out of all this. I should set down the fact that the founder of this firm, Joseph Malaby Dent, died in 1925, and that the first editor of Everyman's Library, Ernest Rhys, died in 1946; that the sales by the year 1952 approached forty millions and that in the year 1956 Everyman's attained its Golden Jubilee and, incidentally, reached its 1000th title which was Aristotle's *Metaphysics*.

The reader must bear with my vanity when I confess to being even more impressed by the fact that my own name is on the title-page of Boswell's *Life of Samuel Johnson*, the two volumes of which were reissued in the new format in 1949 with a new introduction by Sir Sydney Roberts and a brand new and greatly extended index—by *me*. They are—allow me to repeat—the first two volumes of Everyman's Library, Nos. 1 and 2, which had first appeared in 1906—when I was a babe of one.

Does the bewildered reader imagine this author has wandered far from the subject of Covent Garden, his own or anyone else's? Not so; we are in Aldine House in Bedford Street. And a dozen yards away, at No. 16 Bedford Street, is the site of the house of Thomas Sheridan, father of Richard Brinsley, the wit and playwright, who had shares in Drury Lane Theatre and saw it burned to the ground on one particular occasion. The house was on the west side, looking directly along Henrietta Street, and Dr Johnson often visited there, as I have already described.

King Street is even richer in historical, literary, musical and histrionic associations than is Henrietta Street. It is called after King Charles I just as its parallel is called after his queen, Henrietta Maria.

James Quin, a fine actor and a great Falstaff whom it took a Garrick to follow and surpass, was born in King Street in 1693. Garrick himself had a lodging there in due course, living from 1743 to 1745 at the house of a cabinet-maker. Let us go westward along the south side, and then eastward along the north side of the street.

There are some dullish buildings and some depressing ones in that they are closed and empty with a notice declaring that the lease is ended (and an implication that the market really is going to move at long last). Hereabouts is a gateway or 'hole in the wall' admitting us to St Paul's Church in its quadrangle. But we pause now to gaze at No. 10, since the poet Coleridge lodged here from 1799 till 1802 when he was quite unknown and writing political articles for *The Morning Post*. We may gaze too—either from within or without—at the tavern called The Essex Serpent, the origin of whose sign was said to be a great dragon which appeared at St Osyth (near Clacton) shortly before the death of King Henry II in 1189. In the middle of the street used to be the storeroom of Messrs Barr who were very famous seed-merchants until a few years ago. Alongside still are the offices of Messrs Curtis Brown, literary agents with a vastly impressive clientele, past and present; they will see to it that you get published all over the wide world if you deserve it. At the end, at No 16, are the offices of the Communist Party of Great Britain and the Young Communist League. These have a somewhat secretive air. Opposite, across Bedford Street, are the spacious warehouses, showrooms and dressing-rooms of Moss Brothers who can attire you for any polite function whatsoever.

But it is the other side of King Street which is much more after my own heart and much more part of my own direct experience. No. 26, the premises of Debenham, Storr and Sons at the corner of King Street and Garrick Street, is a strange, tall Italianate building (approved by architectural historians) belonging to a firm of property salesmen which has been there since 1813. The present building dates from 1860. The only time I entered this building—it was quite by chance and whim—I found myself in the midst of a desultory sale of stage-scenery belonging to the late Sir John Martin-Harvey—the scenery, as I remember, of plays such as *The Breed of the Treshams* and *The Only Way*. It was so much like being behind the scenes of any theatre in the daytime and the daylight that I beat a hasty retreat. That was less than a dozen years ago; I must go back soon, before it is too late. Next door at No. 27 is a handsome building, with a Royal coat-of-arms superimposed, which declares itself to belong to 'The Westminster Fire Office: established 1717'. I am told that this is the original building, and that early insurance offices did not use the word 'insurance'—as this does not.

No 29 is the dignified but un-historical headquarters of Rank Strand Electric, a company which excels itself in everything to do with stage-lighting, as well as of every other sort of lighting. This organization haunts me, and obsesses me. For example, around 1950 I went to Turkey to lecture in Istanbul, Ankara and Izmir on the filming of Shakespeare—one week in each city. It was no great surprise to find in Ankara the well-known picture of Dr Arne, composer of *Rule, Britannia* and much else, hanging in the headquarters of the British Council, which was my host on this trip. But it was more than a surprise, one day later—a surprise revealing the universality of Covent Garden—to go to Ankara Opera House and be shown with great pride and by the manager himself the new electric console, overlooking the stage from the back of what we used to call the dress-circle. A splendid object not at all unlike an exceedingly grand grand-piano. And above the keyboard was the inscription: STRAND ELECTRIC—29 KING STREET, COVENT GARDEN, LONDON, ENGLAND. It had been installed the previous year by Mr Bear, an old friend of mine, who has since then told me more than once how much he enjoyed his trip to Turkey.

The next two or three numbers in King Street were occupied—and still are, more or less, occupied—by market salesmen whom I know well, and who know me well, by sight. At No 33, the shop and offices of Messrs Barrow Brothers, I dwelt for ten years on the top floor—from about 1935 till about 1945. It was not much of an apartment—three smallish rooms and a clothes-cupboard in all. It was not really an apartment at all—just a converted office, with at the back a balcony space in the open air, for plants and window-boxes on the ledge, as one wished. This I called the 'loggia', a title to which the square-yard or so was not entitled. Or, sometimes, the hacienda! But in these rooms, over that ten years, I spent some of my happiest hours, and minutes, and mornings, and nights. Any chronicle of my life there belongs to my autobiography, not to this book.

But what is most relevant is that, at this same number and address,

33 King Street, lived George Frederick Cooke in the year 1795. To be Edmund Kean's favourite actor is to be something, and Cooke was just that. He had been a kind of harbinger of Kean himself. In the London season of 1800 he had made a sensation as Richard III, in which character Kean was to make an even greater sensation in 1814. Cooke was great, also, as Shylock, Iago and Sir Giles Overreach. But he died in America, worn out with dissipation, in 1812. He was the first great English actor to tour in America, and when Kean was there twelve years later and was surrounded with troubles of his own, he moved ecclesiastical mountains to raise a monument to Cooke's memory. That was in 1821. Writing of Cooke's death, Kean's biographer says: 'Perhaps the times were not ripe, perhaps he needed a Hazlitt. . . .' It is a great compliment to a great critic.

In the dozen yards between No. 33 and No. 43, between my ex-residence and the still extant ex-mansion where our tour comes to an end, there is almost too much to record as having happened. Next door was born Dr Thomas Augustine Arne *and* his sister who became Mrs Cibber, the actress and singer who sang in the first-ever performance of Handel's *Messiah* which was in Dublin in the year 1742. Arne's own *Masque of Alfred* (containing that not unfamiliar air, *Rule, Britannia*) was almost certainly composed in King Street and had its first performance in 1740 at Cliveden before Frederick, Prince of Wales. At No. 35 was the original Garrick Club (1831) whose history I have already sketched. Its pilastered windows on the first floor have survived and are to be noted.

But this same address has a further and still older theatrical connection: 'We fear there will be found a dearth of good comic gentry, and lovers. Oh Lewis! where art thou for the fops and flutterers, with thy person almost as light as thy voice, thy winking eyes, and little teeth-shewing laugh! And where art thou, Elliston, the best lover we ever saw in a comedy, for in the midst of vigorous gaiety thy voice could tremble with emotion, and no actor *approached* a woman as thou didst, fervid, and as if she really attracted thee? Thy raptures are not at arm's length, at the tip-end of a white glove.' Thus Leigh Hunt, writing about the imminent season at Drury Lane in 1830 and invoking the memory of two of the excellent old actors—Covent-Gardeners both—who had either passed on or retired from action. Lewis, a most mercurial player, lived for some years at 35 King Street, before the original Garrick Club was founded there.

To No. 37, in the early sixties of this present century, came the Savage Club for a few years; in 1968 it set up house with the Constitutional Club in Northumberland Avenue. At No. 38 were the rooms of Samuel Paterson, a celebrated literary auctioneer to whose youngest son Dr Samuel Johnson (the inescapable) was godfather. At this same address in the same century Charles Dibdin first set up an entertainment (largely solo) of his own devising. He called it London Amusement and in this he sang his own song (*Poor Jack*) to his own music, and made it his most popular ditty; though it may not have lasted so well as *Tom Bowling* and *The Lass that Loved a Sailor*, both again wholly his own work, like hundreds of other songs almost exclusively nautical. All of them, for me, are full of a breezy charm alternating with a salt-water pathos. They are, I suppose, utterly out of fashion nowadays. But for me they will never go *out*. It is said that Dibdin never went to sea, except for a day or two. (We have already had a glimpse of him on dry land—at the other end of the Market.) But his achievement in writing so many ballads that are so utterly nautical, both in tune and in sentiment, is all the more worthy of note and of praise.

We are now come to the offices of a very successful and long-established firm of fruit importers, Messrs George Monro, Ltd, and, just beyond these, No 43 King Street, the old mansion which the same firm has taken over. But this is so important an edifice, so rich in history, that I propose to leave its consideration to the last pages of this book. And I propose, meanwhile, to cross King Street, go through the 'hole in the wall' close to No 10, and give myself and my readers a rest in St Paul's Church and the graveyard that is now a garden in the middle of Covent Garden. It should be mentioned, as we cross the road, that both the old church and the old mansion (of many names) are conspicuously to be seen in Hogarth's 'Morning' when they were both already a century old. Not quite so conspicuous as the withered beldame with the smirk in the central foreground; but that was the way with the eighteenth century!

The most often repeated story about the church is the story of its building by Inigo Jones. When the Earl of Bedford commissioned the young architect to build a church in the middle of the district, he said, or is said to have said: 'We are farmers, so build us a barn to worship in.' And Inigo Jones built St Paul's Church, Covent Garden and said to the owner of the whole district: 'I have built you the handsomest barn in England.' There are plenty of far more beautiful churches in England. I would even dare to say that there are plenty of far more beautiful barns. But it is only fair to add that it looks much handsomer—and distinctly more ecclesiastical—in old prints, and to point out that the church has been at least once—if not twice—gutted by fire and reconstructed since the seventeenth century. It has lost its short steeple, and its former back porch has become its only entrance (Pl. 40).

It must be taken as a purely personal opinion if I say that this is a church neither to pray nor to worship in, primarily, but rather one in which to muse on mortality. It is more of a graveyard than a temple. Best to give one's own list of eight outstanding persons whose remains lie here and to set them down in order of quality rather than of calling:

ELLEN TERRY—English goddess among great actresses

DR ARNE—illustrious national-anthemist

SIR PETER LELY—colourful depicter of kings, queens and royal mistresses

CHARLES MACKLIN—oldest of our old actors (who died at nearly 100)

GRINLING GIBBONS—most exquisite of carvers in wood and stone

THOMAS GIRTIN—prince of water-colourists

WILLIAM WYCHERLEY—most brutally witty among Restoration playwrights

EDWARD KYNASTON—who played Juliet to Betterton's Romeo before women were allowed to act.

They call it 'The Actors' Church' and with good reason: on the back wall are thirteen panels inscribed with the names of thirteen luminaries of the drama, the dance and the lighter stage in our own time. They run in alphabetical order: Charles Blake Cochran, Jose Collins, Clemence Dane, Edouard Espinosa, Sophie Feodorovich, Leslie Henson, Baliol Holloway, Vivien Leigh, Ivor Novello, W. Macqueen-Pope, Leon Quartermaine, Ada Reeve, Bransby Williams.

Now, as I have said, I must return to what is in many ways the most interesting building in the whole market—the house at one time simply called The Star Coffee House and now called George Monro's. It is No. 43 King Street, almost in the Piazza, a stately building still, and some even call it the most notable building in the whole neighbourhood (Pl. 38). It preserves its old façade, that of a fine town-house built in 1636. Another London perambulator, Beresford Chancellor, goes so far as to call it 'the principal architectural feature in Covent Garden' and 'doubtless one of Inigo Jones's creations'; he also points out the curious fact that it seldom seems to have had a definite name or to have borne one name for very long. Its first resident was William Alexander, Earl of Stirling, the Scottish statesman and poet who was created an earl in 1633. In 1626 he was appointed Secretary of State for Scotland, and he died, presumably in this his London house, in 1640. He was a friend of William Drummond of Hawthornden and was himself a poet good enough to have one poem in Q's *Oxford Book of English Verse* and to survive, though faintly, in other anthologies.

The second tenant was Thomas Killigrew, a real Restoration roustabout and a leading figure in the theatre of his time. He had been a page in the household of King Charles I, and afterwards a companion of King Charles II in exile and his Groom of the Bed-chamber after the Restoration. Born in 1612, he had published by 1664 no fewer than nine indifferent plays written, he tells us, in nine different cities. He was for some time manager of the King's Company at the Theatre Royal, Drury Lane, a theatre with which his own career was intimately connected. As manager he was the first to obtain permission for women to take female parts on the stage. In the year 1660 he and Sir William Davenant were granted patents by the King to build two new playhouses and 'to raise two new companies of players, and to have the sole regulation thereof'. In documents of about this time he is referred to as 'Thomas Killigrew of Covent Garden, Esq.'—a proud title. Later, along with the principal actors of his own company, he obtained from the Earl of Bedford a lease for forty-one years of a piece of ground lying in the parishes of St Martin-in-the-Fields and St Paul's, Covent Garden, which was known by the name of the Riding Yard. On this he built the first Theatre Royal, Drury Lane, which he opened on 8th April 1663 with Beaumont and Fletcher's *The Humorous Lieutenant*. His own play, *The Parson's Wedding*, was put on at the same new theatre by an all-female cast and is said to have been of an obscenity that made even Samuel Pepys blush. If we look into Pepys's Diary in order to find the authority for this legend we find only this non-committal and equivocal description of a visit to Pepys by Peter Luellin, a clerk of the Council: 'He tells me what a bawdy play this *Parson's Wedding* is, that is acted by nothing but women at the King's house, and I am glad of it.' Elsewhere Killigrew is called by Pepys 'a merry droll', and he was unofficial jester as well as official Master of the Revels to the King. He had apartments in Whitehall after he left King Street, and there he died in 1683.

The next resident of the great house in King Street was Sir Kenelm Digby (already discovered in Aubrey), the naval commander and diplomatist whose father was executed for his share in the Gunpowder Plot. Digby was an extraordinary mixture of the genuine scientist and the mountebank. He was an astrologer, an alchemist, a biologist and a quack. He was a man of great credulity who was also several times described as a consummate liar. He enjoyed having scientific men to visit him at Covent Garden, and he often wrangled there with the philosopher Thomas Hobbes. Digby has been described as an irresponsible but versatile man, and one abounding in intellectual curiosity. But his critics regarded him as a humbug.

Admiral Russell, Lord Orford, who defeated the French off Cape La Hogue in 1692, resided here till his death in 1727. He left the house to Thomas, Lord Archer, who lived here with his father-in-law, James West. This last was a great bookseller and President of the Royal Society. He died in this house in 1772, and here was sold his great collection of books and prints, coins and medals. These were so numerous that the sale lasted for nearly six weeks.

In 1774 the house was converted into the first 'family hotel' established in London. In 1790 it came into the hands of W. C. Evans and became known as Evans's Hotel and Evans's Supper Rooms. The name Evans was retained by many of his successors, and one of these, John Green—familiarly known as Paddy Green—built a hall in what had been Lord Orford's garden, which became a famous and popular haunt for suppers with music. Many good singers and instrumentalists performed there, including Paddy Green (himself a good singer) and Sam Cowell, who excelled in ballads that were lurid and gruesome. Among the devoted frequenters of Evans's were Thackeray and Douglas Jerrold, Serjeants Murphy and Ballantine, Lionel Lawson and George Augustus Sala, John Leech and Henry Mayhew. To these may be added the drama critic Clement Scott, the *Punch* editor Sir Francis Burnand, and such all-round journalists and men-of-the-theatre as Edmund Yates and George R. Sims. Quoting from many of these, the late Harold Scott has given us a good composite picture of what an evening at Evans's, *late* Joy's, was like. His book, *The Early Doors*, is a history of the early music-hall; it was published during the

paper shortage at the end of the Second World War, and its flimsy
appearance was one of the reasons why it had never anything like the
success its thoroughness and enthusiasm deserved:

'Midnight, "when all the girls were home", was the correct
time at which to arrive. In Paddy Green's days, when the larger
room had been built, entering down the two or three steps which
are still to be seen, one made one's way through the smaller room
to the Hall, where at long tables groups of gentlemen were to be
seen, taking supper and listening, or half listening, to the efforts of
the entertainers on the large platform at the end of the room, which
was flanked by Corinthian pillars, backed by a large apse, and
supported a grand piano and a harmonium. Much has been made
of the food consumed at Evans's, and it is important, for appreciation of its atmosphere, to remember that the place was essentially a
cabaret in which entertainment was incidental to refreshment.
There is a consensus of opinion that the food supplied was good,
and that the prices charged for it were high. The style of the menu
was that of the high-class chop house. Favourite dishes were
poached eggs on steak and devilled kidneys seasoned with red
pepper. The baked potatoes in their jackets inspired poems in their
day, and the brown ale, porter, stout and brandy—served to the
clients in those happy times at all hours of the night—enjoyed their
full share of literary appreciation. There are records of a "calcula-
ting waiter" who bluffed the more unsuspecting customers by the
rapidity with which he concocted a fictitious reckoning, and who
was enshrined as an institution . . . [Many] have written of the
"homeliness," comfort and good-fellowship of Evans's, of its
Attic wit, and of its camaraderie, and there can be no doubt that
in the best years they enjoyed themselves there. The mental picture
afforded by the many descriptions of the place is not unpleasing.
The lofty hall, with its chaste neo-Grecian embellishments, the
tables humming with conversation—(this in spite of the adjuration
printed on the green-covered programme booklets that "Gentlemen
are respectfully requested to encourage the vocalists by attention;
the café parts of the room being intended for conversational
parties")—and old Van Joel [described as a kind of resident
buffoon with a trick of jumping up unexpectedly] doddering round
the hall selling the cigars which all commentators take relish in

describing as bad, and telling the purchasers that, upon a date not yet fixed, he is giving a benefit concert, and will they kindly purchase a ticket?'

The nightly entertainment was in two parts. First the choir-boys from the Savoy Chapel sang their glees and part-songs, the words of which were printed in the green programmes with more or less learned notes. These choral numbers, interspersed with two or three solo performances, made up the more responsible or introductory section. The real fun of the evening began when the comic vocalists, usually led by the redoubtable Sam Cowell, arrived on the animated scene. Cowell was the man who mattered most here, for years and years. An American by birth, he had come to central London by way of Scotland. Harold Scott classed him as a master-entertainer with Dan Leno and Arthur Roberts: 'His voice was round, clear, and well-produced. His power of mimicry was considerable, and, an actor before everything, he penetrated the characters he presented while retaining that mysterious "plus" of personality without which no entertainer can make his special type of effect.'

Sam Cowell was the father of a well-known actress who called herself, in somewhat unusual style, Mrs A. B. Tapping, and played for years with Mr and Mrs Kendal. I never saw Mrs Tapping, who died early in 1926. But I heard and read much of her high melodramatic quality from my seniors in criticism, and I saw her daughter, Sydney Fairbrother, a dozen times at least. Though Sydney died as long ago as 1941, I can still easily see in my mind's eye her high melodramatic features, her deeply lined face, her baleful eyes, even when she played, as she usually did, a mildly comic part or in an immensely successful music-hall sketch with Fred Emney. For me she was always a relic of the last century, and I never saw her without thinking of her illustrious pedigree. The audiences at Evans's never wearied of Sam Cowell singing dramatic songs such as *Billy Barlow* and *The Ratcatcher's Darter*. His nightly appearance, however late, was always greeted with an ovation. Nor was he one of those public favourites who tend to go on for ever, or to say farewell for a decade at least. Sam Cowell died at forty-four in 1864.

Other memorable performers at Evans's include J. W. Sharpe, W. G. Ross, Harry Sydney, and Sam Collins, who has left his name in Collins's Music-Hall in Islington and the title of whose best-known song, *The Rocky Road to Dublin*, is still a kind of household word. Only the very superior person will smile at Sam Collins's epitaph:

> A loving husband and a faithful friend,
> Ever the first a helping hand to lend;
> Farewell, good-natured, honest-hearted Sam,
> Until we meet before the GREAT I AM.

Another regular singer at Evans's was Harry Clifton, who sang intensely wholesome songs for which he is said to have written his own words as well as his own music—like Harry Lauder long after him. Each of his songs was separately published, usually with a coloured photogravure cover of Harry Clifton himself with his benign and honest countenance. I treasured these in my childhood, and I have some of them—somewhere—still. Harry Clifton's songs were bracingly wise and moral, with titles such as *Work, Boys, Work, and Be Contented* and *Paddle Your Own Canoe*. Harold Scott's comment on Clifton is, I am glad to see, not in the least scornful: 'Songs such as *Work, Boys, Work* and *Always Put Your Shoulder To The Wheel* must have given great satisfaction to those members of his audience who were employers of labour; but it is a part of the strange psychology of music-hall audiences that this kind of sentiment is invariably well received in the gallery.'

Coon songs, sung as often as not to banjo accompaniment, also became popular in those early days which may almost be called pre-music-hall. Today's young folk, who fondly imagine that a show like the 'coloured' revue which recently ran for endless months in Victoria has anything particularly novel about it, fondly imagine a vain thing. Harold Scott traces such minstrel shows back to at least 1840: 'It is known on unimpeachable testimony that these artists brought tears to the spectacles of William Makepeace Thackeray.'

Ladies—of any sort—were not admitted at Evans's until the late sixties, and then an Act of Parliament of 1872 forbade licence of any sort of entertainment after 12.30 a.m. This gave the final blow, the essence of Evans's programmes being that they took place in the early hours of the morning. 'Evans's Late Joys' were no more. They had been happily so called because Evans took over from a previous manager called Joy, with the result that a sign was put up calling the place 'Evans's—Late Joy's', The transition in nomenclature to the title 'Evans's Late Joys' was natural and easy.

Almost sixty years passed in the course of which the building's ground floor became known for a time as King's Hall (which had its irregular career as a theatre—of which more later) and thereafter as the headquarters of the National Sporting Club (where many distinguished prize-fights took place presided over by Lord Lonsdale and his vast, imposing cigar). Then, in 1930, a delicate and charming young actor called Peter Ridgeway appeared in Hampstead in a play about Charles Lamb written by Miss Joan Temple. In this play, entitled *Charles and Mary*, the playwright herself acted inspiredly as Charles's sister Mary. Incidentally, Lamb's father was memorably played by Harold Scott, whose book I have been liberally quoting. The play was a gentle little masterpiece, and among its critics my old chief James Agate—departing for once in a way from his habitual brusque dismissal—gave the play and its performance a gentle little masterpiece of a notice which must have given the production the most helpful sort of encouragement. It was at once promoted to the Globe Theatre, where it did as well as a gentle masterpiece could be expected to do. *Charles and Mary* was revived in 1930 at the Players' Theatre Club, again with Miss Temple as Mary Lamb and Peter Ridgeway as Charles, and in its new home it again did very well.

But where, the reader may ask, was this new home called The Players' Theatre Club? It was on the top floor of the same remarkable old mansion which had been the dwelling of a dozen celebrities in turn, then a hotel of a sort, then a tavern, then the Star Coffee House, then the headquarters of Evans's Late Joys which had been Evans's Song and Supper Rooms. Then it was the King's Hall, then the National Sporting Club, then the offices of a great firm of fruit importers with, on the top floor, a new cabaret-theatre which called itself Ridgeway's Late Joys. This gradually developed into that Victorian music-hall which moved during the Second World War to Albemarle Street and is now prosperously installed in the old Gatti Music-Hall Building in Villiers Street, Charing Cross. In its earliest shape—at King Street—I saw some of the earliest appearances in burlesque of such new young artists as Alec Clunes, Robert Eddison and Peter Ustinov, and did all in my power to encourage them as very promising skylarkers in that upper floor.

The building has yet another claim to fame. Our two veteran Dames of the theatre both played in it once when it was the King's Hall, on the ground floor. Dame Sybil Thorndike made an amateur appearance here as Gloria in Shaw's *You Never Can Tell* in 1905. Dame Edith Evans played Cressida here in a William Poel production of Shakespeare's *Troilus and Cressida* in 1912, her first appearance on any stage. Among those present on the latter occasion was George Moore, who afterwards told dramatic critics, absent on this occasion, to look out for this new young actress in the future. These two débuts give the great old building a claim to perpetuity as well as to fame.

Let me add here a very personal reminiscence of my own. It concerns what was infinitely the proudest and most exciting ten minutes of my twenty-months career as a Sick Berth Attendant in the Royal Navy. This occurred some time in 1944 when I was deputed to convey Edmund Kean's sword as Richard III from the stage-door of the Haymarket Theatre to the stage-door of the New Theatre. It was a gift from John Gielgud to Laurence Olivier on the occasion of the latter's Richard. I was, of course, in uniform, and the sword, in its scabbard of red and gold, I carried laid across my extended arms, like a babe carried to a christening font. If I met any 'gold-braid' on my journey I did not deign to notice it, and it would anyhow have been too startled and flabbergasted to expect any salute or recognition, war-time or not.

POSTSCRIPT

Sir Bronson Albery died in July 1971, at the great age of ninety. He owned among other theatres both the New and Wyndham's which stand back to back between St Martin's Lane and the Charing Cross Road. At the beginning of the year 1973 the name of the New was happily changed to the Albery as a tribute to his memory. This must have gratified the great old man, and he would have been no less gratified to know that the play still successfully running when the New became the Albery was a revival of Dion Boucicault's 130-year-old comedy, *London Assurance*, in which Sir Bronson's famous step-father, Sir Charles Wyndham, used to enjoy playing the charming adventurer called Dazzle. My book is dedicated to Sir Bronson's gracious memory.

END-PIECE

The last word on the subject of Covent Garden should go to, and come from, Thackeray. For that great novelist and London-lover (1811–63) enjoyed and revelled in Covent Garden as much as—probably more than—all the countless porters and salesmen, and club-members, writers and painters, actors and draughtsmen, men about and around the town and the theatre, who for the past three hundred years have worked and played and lived there to the top of the hilt. It was Thackeray who, in a superbly comprehensive passage, caught the place's very essence:

'The two great national theatres on one side,; a churchyard full of mouldy and undying celebrities on the other; a fringe of houses studded in every part with anecdote and history; an arcade, often more gloomy and deserted than a cathedral aisle; a rich cluster of brown old taverns—one of them [The Garrick Club?] filled with the counterfeit presentments of many actors long since silent who scowl or smile once more from the canvas upon the grandsons of their dead admirers; a something in the air which breathes of old books, old pictures, old painters, and old authors; a place beyond all other places one would choose in which to hear the chimes at midnight; a crystal palace—the representation of the present— which peeps timidly from a corner upon many things in the past; a withered bank that has been sucked dry by a fabulous clerk; a squat building with a hundred columns and chapel-looking fronts, which always stand knee-deep in baskets, flowers and scattered vegetables; a common centre into which nature showers her choicest gifts, and where the kindly fruits of the earth often nearly choke the narrow thoroughfares; a population that never seems to sleep, and

163

that does all in its power to prevent others sleeping; a place where
the very latest suppers and the earliest breakfasts jostle each other on
the footways—such is Covent Garden Market, with some of its
surrounding features.'

Yet it should be said finally—for even to Thackeray cannot be
vouchsafed the very last word on a subject so dear to me—that there
exists somewhere in this Covent Garden, which is in the dead middle
of the heart of London, the tallest office in all the world of Messrs
Hearsay & Surmise, who have an office in every capital and whose
two chief clerks are called Fake and Fancy. Within that old unvener-
able London mansion—reputed once to have been the home of the
Minister of Misinformation—this celebrated firm of history-makers
and news-inventors and scandalmongers have their busy headquarters,
with teeming staircases and whispering corridors. The vats of rumour
and the spite of spiders are susurrant all over this imagined edifice. It
is an establishment which will continue to prosper and flourish when
Covent Garden Market itself has been reinstated miles away, and
when ultimately the great theatres of the district, the banqueting-halls
of drama and music, the long-standing houses and offices of good and
ill fame, even the Piazza and even the Churches, and all things else in
these hallowed and unhallowed fields, are flattened in a matter of
seconds, and laid bare and waste for evermore.

BOOKS AND JOURNALS CONSULTED

BAGNOLD, Enid, *Autobiography*. Heinemann, 1969.

BARTON, Margaret, *Garrick*. Faber and Faber, 1948.

BAX, Clifford, *Pretty, Witty Nell: Nell Gwynn and Her Environment*. Chapman and Hall, 1932.

BONE, James, *The London Perambulator*. Jonathan Cape, 1925.

BOSWELL, James, *The London Journal, 1762–1763*. Heinemann, 1950.
Boswell in Search of a Wife, 1766–1769. Heinemann, 1957.
Boswell for the Defence, 1769–1774. Heinemann, 1960.
Boswell: The Ominous Years, 1774–1776. Heinemann, 1963.

CAMPBELL, Mrs Patrick, *My Life and Some Letters*. Hutchinson, 1922.

CARDUS, Neville (ed.), *Kathleen Ferrier—A Memoir*. Hamish Hamilton, 1954.

Chambers's Encyclopaedia.

CHANCELLOR, E. Beresford. *The Annals of Covent Garden and its Neighbourhood*. Hutchinson, 1930.

COHEN-PORTHEIM, Paul, *The Spirit of London*. Batsford, 1935.

CUNNINGHAM, George H., *London: A Comprehensive Survey*. J. M. Dent, 1927.

Dictionary of National Biography.

DISHER, M. Willson, *Melodrama*. Rockcliff, 1954.

DORAN, Dr John, *Their Majesties' Servants*. 1864.

HAZLITT, William, *Collected Works*. J. M. Dent, 1903.

House of Dent, The, J. M. Dent, 1938.

JACOBS, Reginald, *Covent Garden, its Romance and History*. Simpkin Marshall, 1913.

LUCAS, E. V., *London*. Methuen, 1926.

Manchester Guardian, The.

MANDER, Raymond, and MITCHENSON, Joe, *The Theatres of London*. Rupert Hart-Davis, 1961.

PATTERSON, Clara Burdett, *Angela Burdett-Coutts and the Victorians*. John Murray, 1953.

PEPYS, Samuel, *Diary*.

POUND, Reginald, *The Strand Magazine 1891–1950*. Heinemann, 1966.

RASMUSSEN, S. E., *London: the Unique City*. Cape, 1937; Penguin Books, 1960.

ROBERTSON, W. Graham, *Time Was*. Hamish Hamilton, 1955.

RUSSELL, William Clark, *Representative Actors*. Warne, 1890.

SCOTT, Harold, *The Early Doors*. Nicholson and Watson, 1946.

SMITH, John Thomas, *Nollekens and his Times*. Turnstile Press Edition, 1948.

SPENCER, Alfred (ed.), *Memoirs of William Hickey* (4 volumes). Hurst and Blackett, 1913–25.

STEELE, Sir Richard, *The Tatler*.

STEEN, Marguerite, *A Pride of Terrys*. Longmans, 1962.

SUMMERSON, Sir John, *Georgian London*. Penguin Books, 1945.

TERRISS, Ellaline, *Just a Little Bit of String*. Hutchinson, 1955.

TERRY, Ellen, *The Story of My Life*. Hutchinson, 1908.

Times, The.

WALKLEY, A. B., *Drama and Life*. Methuen, 1907.

WHYTE, Samuel, *Miscellanea Nova*. 1801.

WILSON, A. E., *The Lyceum*. Dennis Yates, 1952.

YOUNG, Elizabeth and Wayland, *Old London Churches*. Faber and Faber, 1956.

INDEX